Stanislavski

Revealed

DIRECTING THE ACTION
by Charles Marowitz

Every actor and director who enters the orbit of this major work will find himself challenged to a deeper understanding of his art and propelled into further realms of exploration. Marowitz meditates on all the sacred precepts of theater practice including auditions, casting, design, rehearsal, actor psychology, dramaturgy and the text.

Directing the Action yields a revised liturgy for all those who would celebrate a theatrical passion on today's stage. But in order to be a disciple in this order, the theater artist must be poised toward piety and heresy at once. Not since Peter Brook's *The Empty Space* has a major director of such international stature confronted the ancient dilemmas of the stage with such a determined sense of opportunity and discovery.

"An enerbizing, uplifting work ... reading Marowitz on theater is like reading heroic fiction in an age without heroes."
—LOS ANGELES WEEKLY

"A cogent and incisive collection of ideas, well formulated and clearly set forth; an important contribution on directing in a postmodern theater."
—CHOICE

"Consistently thought-provoking ... Sure to be controversial."
—LIBRARY JOURNAL

paper • ISBN: 1-55783-072-X

ACTING IN FILM
An Actor's Take on Moviemaking
by Michael Caine

"*Remarkable material . . . A treasure . . . I'm not going to be looking at performances quite the same way . . . A grand entertainment with more drama than most movies . . . He's a marvelous teacher . . . A real clear-cut lesson that every critic should see and everybody who goes to the movies should see . . . Fascinating!*" —GENE SISKEL, SISKEL & EBERT

"*Witty, articulate and always entertaining, Michael Caine takes the nuts and bolts of film acting to pieces and gives away more trade secrets in the process than you thought existed.*" —GEOFFREY HOBBS, THE SUNDAY TIMES

"*Wonderful reading . . . Caine's guidance, aimed at novices still dreaming of the big break, can also give hardened critics fresh insights.*" —CHARLES CHAMPLIN, LOS ANGELES TIMES

"*Caine knows so much, not just about acting, but about the whole business of filmmaking. Don't think of this as too esoteric or for actors only. You'll be laughing, absorbed and enchanted.*" —ELIZABETH COWLEY, THE DAILY MAIL

"*No one is more qualified to discuss the craft and business of film acting . . . An insider's look of as much interest to members of the audience as to actors.*" —ALLEN BARRA, THE NEW YORK TIMES BOOK REVIEW

cloth • Over 30 stills • ISBN: 0-936839-86-4 • $14.95
video • 60 minutes • ISBN: 1-55783-034-7 • $39.95

THE APPLAUSE ACTING SERIES

Stanislavski Revealed

The Actor's Guide to Spontaneity on Stage

■ ■ ■

by

Sonia Moore

Author of
The Stanislavski System

APPLAUSE
THEATRE BOOKS

STANISLAVSKI REVEALED
The Actor's Guide to Spontaneity on Stage

This is a revised, updated and expanded edition of *Training an
Actor*.

Library of Congress Cataloging-in-Publication Data

Moore, Sonia.
  Stanislavski revealed : the actor's guide to spontaneity on stage
  / by Sonia Moore. -- 1st Applause ed.
      p.   cm. -- (The Applause acting series)
    Rev. ed. of: Training an actor, 1979.
    Includes bibliographical references.
    ISBN 1-55783-103-3 (trade paper) : $9.95
    1. Acting -- Study and teaching. 2. Method (Acting) I. Moore,
  Sonia. Training an actor. II. Title. III. Series.
PN2062.M62. 1991   91-28205
792'.028'07 -- dc20   CIP

Applause Theatre Books
211 West 71st Street
New York, NY 10023
Phone 212-595-4735, Fax 212-721-2856

First Applause Edition: 1991
Second Applause Edition, 1998

"Not long before his death, Stanislavski developed the basis of theatre art. He determined the essence of his teaching as 'The Method of Physical Actions.' This method is now the only one, and there is nothing to equal it in the field of an actor's art that existed or exists in the world theatre."

—G.A. Tovstonogov
Artistic Director of the Leningrad
Bolshoi Dramatic Theatre

"Without the Method of Physical Actions, there is no Stanislavski System."

—P.V. Simonov
The Method of Konstantin Stanislavski
and Physiology of Emotions Moscow, "Nauka," 1962, p. 15

"With the Method of Physical Actions, Stanislavski established the beginning of science of theatre art and opened the perspective of scientifically proven theatre education."

—P.V. Simonov, neurophysiologist
and P.M. Ershov, theatre scholar and director
Temperament Character Personality
Moscow, "Nauka," 1964, p. 109

"An actor plays well only when his behavior is subordinated to natural organic laws of creativity which are rooted in human nature. Great actors achieved this spontaneously. This happened before the Stanislavski System. The System is the practical teaching of natural organic laws of creativity. Therefore whenever an actor plays well, convincingly, sincerely, he always plays according to the Stanislavski System—whether he did it consciously or unconsciously, acted intentionally or was subordinated to his talent, to the demands of mother nature itself."

—B.E. Zakhava, Director
Dean of the Schukin School
at the Vakhtangov Theatre
in *Eugene Vakhtangov*
Moscow VTO, 1984, p. 482

This text is based on tape recordings from Sonia Moore's classes at her studio. The transcripts have been edited, compressed, and, in many instances, revised.
The students are composites, their names fictitious.
Their questions and responses are typical of those learning Stanislavski's final technique.

CONTENTS

Introduction... 1

Class 1 13

Class 2 27

Class 3 38

Class 4 50

Class 5 64

Class 6 80

Class 7 90

Class 8 108

Class 9 124

Class 10 137

Class 11 154

Class 12 165

Suggested Exercises

    Relaxation of Muscles 169

    Silent Exercises and Improvisation 179

    Sense Memory Exercises 183

    Exercises with Imaginary Objects 185

    Exercises for Images 187

    Tempo-Rhythm Exercises 188

    Oral Exercises and Improvisations 189

Bibliography 193

A Brief Chronology of Stanislavski 195

■ Introduction

Konstantin Stanislavski, the great Russian actor, director, and reformer of the theatre, spent his life searching for the secret of inspiration. A brilliant actor, Stanislavski surrounded himself with a company of geniuses. In his company's productions, and in the performances of the great European actors of the late nineteenth and early twentieth centuries, Stanislavski observed that it was inspiration that raised an actor to the height of his art. When an actor is inspired his emotions flow, his actions are real and theatrical, his performance is clear to the audience; in short, the actor reincarnates himself as the character.

Stanislavski also observed that inspiration is an infrequent visitor, even to actors of genius. An actor, he noted, is forced to pretend, to push emotions, and, as a result, gives a mediocre, "uninspired" performance.

Stanislavski believed that theatre has a powerful influence on people and that its responsibility is to bring important ideas to life in great plays. He realized that a play's intent—what he called the superobjective—is not projected when actors do not function on stage as living human beings. Stanislavski's mission in the theatre thus became the pursuit and analysis of inspiration on stage so that any capable actor might exert conscious control over it.

Stanislavski spent more than forty years probing the mystery of inspiration. What should be done to make an actor function on stage naturally, as we do in life? How can an actor control his subconscious mechanism of emotions? An actor must create a functioning human being; actors speak of "building a character." But do they know what to build? For clues Stanislavski turned not only to masters of the theatre but also to psychologists and neurophysiologists.

Early in the development of his system, Stanislavski isolated different elements of human behavior—such as "concentration of attention," "relaxation," "sense memory"—in the belief that mastery of any one of these elements alone might bring the actor into a creative, spontaneous state. His emotions would flow as part of a thoroughly organic natural performance. To that end, Stanislavski developed important exercises. Although progressive and helpful, these exercises did not produce a natural performance. Control of just one element of human behavior did not stir an actor's emotions, nor did it bring him into a natural state.

Stanislavski still faced a great problem: how to bring out an actor's emotions within the circumstances of a play. In life we experience emotions—love, hate, joy, anger—because they are stirred by real causes. But on stage nothing is real; everything is invention. And the actor is well aware of it. An actor who plays Hamlet knows that the actor who plays Claudius did not kill his father; the actor who plays Claudius may be a nice man. Why should he hate him?

Emotion on stage is different from emotion in life because an actor leads a dual existence on stage. He exists as the character but also as the actor who creates the character. Stage emotions must be true, but their quality is changed, Stanislavski said, into a "poetic reflection of life's emotions." The actor on stage lives a "repeated" emotion, not a "primary" emotion. A repeated emotion does not arise from an actual cause; the actor can stir it because he has experienced an analogous emotion in his own life many times. The nerves that repeatedly participate in the experience of this one emotion become highly sensitive.

Unlike a primary emotion, a repeated emotion does not absorb the actor entirely. When a tragedy occurs, we are completely absorbed at the moment; but when we remember this tragedy in a few years, other interests penetrate the experience and make it different. This is the actor's state on stage. The actor who sincerely lives the life of the character never forgets that he is the actor who performs it. Stanislavski said: "Time is an excellent filter, an excellent purifier of memories of emotions once experienced. Moreover, time is an excellent artist. It not only purifies, but is capable of poeticizing memories."

The actor possesses all the emotions he needs before he enters the stage, preserved in what Stanislavski called the "emotional memory." According to Stanislavski, "From many preserved traces of what was experienced, one big, condensed, magnified memory of emotions of the same nature is formed. There is nothing superfluous in such a memory, only the very essence. This is the synthesis of all emotions of the same kind. It does not refer to a small, separate, private instance, but to all those of the same nature."

Once he had discovered the importance of emotional

memory, Stanislavski's experiments became purely psychological. His actors arrived at the theatre hours before curtain time to isolate themselves and to concentrate on a personal tragedy. In rehearsals, actors sat around a table for months discussing the play in an effort to understand the psychology of the characters.

But after years of sitting around tables in deep analysis of various plays, Stanislavski conceded that instead of freeing up emotions, he had actually paralyzed the actor's subconscious. When actors were asked to go on stage and apply what they had learned while talking around the table, "the actors," Stanislavski said, "were walking around with swollen heads but could not play anything." Stanislavski saw the appearance of a new cliché: pretending naturalness, pretending the experience of an emotion. Anyone who looked effortless was considered to be an actor. But acting is not just walking around and showing "naturalness."

Acting must be connected with the play. If an actor does not prepare his character's behavior in harmony with the world of the playwright, his work has nothing to do with the character or the play. Fitting every role to oneself does not help to project the play; it produces dead theatre.

Emotional memory is a vital part of an actor's art. Stanislavski's early experiments in emotional memory, however, actually brought actors to the point of hysteria and affected their nervous systems. This stage of Stanislavski's work has been recognized in Russia as the most dangerous period in the history of the Moscow Art Theatre.

American, European, and indeed Russian theatre experts have been acquainted with Stanislavski's work at different stages of its development. The theatre leader who became acquainted with Stanislavski's teachings when he was working on relaxation was absolutely certain that the secret to the "system" was relaxation. Another, who became acquainted with Stanislavski during his imagination period, went home to teach "imagination" as the magic key to the Stanislavski System. And the one who learned about Stanislavski's use of the emotional memory thought that he knew the system's full and true nature.

In each case, one period of Stanislavski's lifelong experiment was considered to be the whole system. Needless to say, conflict and confusion erupted around the world about the essence and goal of Stanislavski's work. (Some have even blamed Stanislavski's translator, Elizabeth Reynolds Hapgood, for the confusion. But this is unfair, since arguments over the Stanislavski System existed in Russia, where no translation was needed!)

Every one of these experimental techniques, though progressive when he began to work with them, ultimately disappointed Stanislavski, because he realized that not one of them alone was sufficient to stir an actor's emotions in the circumstances of the play. And so Stanislavski continued his search for the "conscious means to the subconscious."

Stanislavski's experiments coincided with the work of the famous Russian neurophysiologist Ivan Pavlov, who was himself investigating the connection between internal experience and its external expression. While it is uncertain what contact, if any, Stanislavski had with Pavlov, they made similar and near-simultaneous discoveries. Like Pavlov, Stanislavski came to the conclusion that the mind and body are so intimately connected that they stimulate and influence each other. Every mental process—every feeling and thought, decision and evaluation—is immediately transmitted through the body in visual expression. Human behavior, in this new light, becomes a continuous, uninterrupted psychophysical process.

In life we think continuously and spontaneously in our circumstances. An actor on stage rarely thinks in the character's circumstances. The actor is worrying about his lines or wondering whether the agent he invited is sitting in the audience. The chaos in the actor's mind creates chaos in his body because his natural psychophysical process has been interrupted. The actor naturally feels uncomfortable and helpless! To pretend "naturalness" he crosses his arms on his chest or puts his hands on his hips, or in his pockets, or he leans on every piece of furniture on stage. His attempt at naturalness results in complete paralysis.

Stanislavski admitted that he had contributed to this paralysis by concentrating exclusively on psychological work. Now, having discerned the powerful connection of mind and body, he began to consider stimulating the physical side of the psychophysical process. The technique he worked on, the Method of Physical Actions, is not just another technical step; it is Stanislavski's legacy to the theatre.

When the actor has mastered the Method of Physical Actions, he goes on stage without trying to force an emotion before he enters. Instead his responsibility is to fulfill a simple, concrete, purposeful physical action. Physical action—not movement. Stanislavski never told an actor to go on stage to simply perform physical movement. Physical movement is a mechanical act. Physical action happens in circumstances; it is dictated by the circumstances. It has its own purpose and psychology. A physical action is the sum total of a complex psychophysical process.

With the Method of Physical Actions, Stanislavski reversed his earlier teachings. He no longer taught that control of one element of human behavior would bring the actor into a creative, spontaneous state; in fact, if any element of nature is missing from a performance, he said, the actor is dead. An actor who assimilates the Method of Physical Actions achieves psychophysical unity and keeps all the elements of human behavior together: emotions are released, the imagination functions, and the actor is concentrated and relaxed.

Stanislavski reversed more than his early beliefs. He reversed the very process of life itself. In life a tragedy happens, we experience an emotion, and our body expresses it. On stage tragedy does not happen; on stage everything is invention. Stanislavski made it possible for an actor to experience an emotion on stage without forcing it by approaching it indirectly through the logic of physical actions.

Some actors and theorists of acting have suggested that any physical movement, even if it is just touching an object on stage, will make an actor "natural." Meyerhold thought that a well-trained body would bring an actor to life. Delsarte's system of "expressive movement" taught actors to express emotions with clichéd gestures prescribed beforehand. Human action on stage depends on numerous factors, such as the specific traits of an individual, the tempo-rhythm of an actor at a particular moment, and the circumstances as established by the playwright. Only purposeful action, expressive of the inner state, will involve the actor's emotions and remain rich in content and fresh in performance. Simply running will not produce fear, as William James proposed; but running from a madman waving a knife rarely fails.

After a brief discussion of the superobjective and major events, the actor using the Method of Physical Actions, investigates the play through improvisations on actions, i.e. the character's behavior. In these improvisations, the actor's mind, his senses, his intuition, the muscles of his body, his whole psychological and physical nature participate. Actors trained in Stanislavski's final technique will reject the use of clichés and concentrate on the revelation of the individual psychology of the character; this technique will bring them to the birth of an organically functioning character on stage.

Late in his life, Stanislavski, in poor health, assembled a group of younger actors and asked them to stage *Tartuffe* to experiment with the Method of Physical Actions. He died during rehearsals, and so never saw his final technique in production.

Stanislavski's discovery has been compared by Russian scientists to the historic discoveries of Newton and Pavlov, yet he did not formulate his final technique in any written treatise. He did not, by any means, record all his thoughts on paper; and what he did write did not satisfy him.

An Actor Prepares is the only text Stanislavski saw published before he died. *Building a Character* was published six years after his death. His complete works, compiled and edited by his colleagues and theatre scholars, weren't finished until 1961.

I have spent my life studying the art of acting. My studies began in 1920 when, after undergoing a rigorous examination, I was accepted to the Moscow Art Theatre's Third Studio. The Studio was directed by Stanislavski's greatest disciple, Eugene Vakhtangov. At that time, of course, Stanislavski had not yet developed the Method of Physical Actions. But since founding my own school and the American Center for Stanislavski Theatre Art, I have searched, studied, and experimented in an effort to arrive at the final and definitive interpretation of the system and to complete our understanding of Stanislavski's legacy to the theatre.

My reading of Russian scientific sources confirms that every emotion—like every other mental process—is linked to specific muscles in our torso. In order to stir an emotion an actor must be capable of finding the muscle to which that emotion is connected. The process requires a great deal of practice, exercise, and experimentation. The actor's body must be trained to achieve the highest degree of sensitivity. Once he has reached that level of psychophysical harmony, a movement of the right muscle will trigger the truthful emotion. The actor will achieve psychophysical involvement; his behavior will be spontaneous, lifelike.

Some authorities claim that a talented actor does not need a technique; they say that a great actor must be born. But a musician and a dancer must also be born with talent. And yet does a great musician or a great dancer achieve virtuosity only through talent? Of course not. To talent, technique must be applied. By the same token, not everyone who studies music for many years will become a great musician; not everyone who studies dance technique for many years will become a great dancer; and not everyone who studies acting technique for many years will become a great actor. But now, a capable actor, with the help of Stanislavski's final technique, can achieve a state of spontaneity that heretofore had been the gift of genius alone. What was possible for only a few elite artists now can be achieved by ensembles of capable actors.

In addition to technique, actors must also strive for culture; they must be educated. The growth of an artist depends on his participation in life. The ability to observe and question is essential to the actor's profession. To build on stage the "life of the human spirit," as Stanislavski called it, an actor must relate to the world around him. He must be interested in current problems. And he must have his own "super-superobjective": his desire to contribute to society with his art. To fulfill such a high responsibility, an actor must have culture and a refined taste. "An artist who has not mastered his profession is a dilettante," Goethe said, "and an artist who has limited himself to his profession is a corpse."

Study and analysis of Stanislavski's legacy continue in Russia today. After three decades of my own work, we at the American Center for Stanislavski Theatre Art have an excellent understanding of the use of this technique. But just as the existence of symphony orchestras or ballet companies is inconceivable without a uniform method of training musicians and dancers, so the effort to build an artistic theatre in America is hopeless without a uniform method of training actors.

We must be dissatisfied with the state of our theatre.

That which was an achievement in the past is now an obstacle in the future. We need new plays that raise moral, psychological, and social questions. Our young playwrights, actors, directors, and theatre scholars must feel the responsibility. They must have the desire to do something important.

There is a very popular notion in America today that we do not have true ensemble acting because we do not have repertory theatres. Ensemble is achieved when actors continually react to one another psychologically and physically. Actors skilled in Stanislavski's final technique will form an ensemble in the first play they perform together. Those who are not trained in this technique will not form an ensemble even after having worked together for twenty years.

The introduction of Stanislavski's early teachings into American theatre was unquestionably beneficial. But it is time to stop accepting Stanislavski's early experiments as the Stanislavski System. It is time that our theatre experts became acquainted with what theatre scholars and scientists in Russia acknowledge to be the heart of the Stanislavski System.

The Stanislavski System is a powerful weapon against dilettantism, against stagnation in the theatre and against distortion of theatre art. It enables the actor to stir in himself the emotions of his character every time he performs. It teaches the dramatist how to construct a play and provides criteria for critics and directors to judge acting and directing. It is the solution to spontaneity on stage and the key to inspiration.

■ Class One

SONIA MOORE: Welcome to the Studio. Our first objective here is to train you as an actor in the most concrete professional acting technique, the Stanislavski System.

The theatre cannot tolerate unskilled actors. An actor is not simply someone who has decided that he is an actor. He is a talented person who has learned how to build and reveal the inner world of the character he portrays on stage. It is through the characters that a playwright projects the meaning of his play. And only actors trained in his final technique are able to create what Stanislavski called the "life of the human spirit." But it is not merely desirable to learn this technique; it is a necessity.

Stanislavski believed that actors were the heart of the theatre, and he imposed tremendous demands on them. The Stanislavski System will be as important to you as the technique and theory of music are to musicians. It is vital for all actors, old and young, for all plays, classic or contemporary, for conventional and unconventional productions, for all nationalities and in all times. We cannot make any of you into another Laurence Olivier or Eleonora Duse, but we can teach you laws that enable you to share their secret. How much you succeed will depend on your talent and diligence.

Your attitude toward your work is just as important

as your talent. You must learn to cooperate, to work for a common objective. It is the group that makes a play into a work of art. An actor who is interested only in his personal success has misunderstood theatre's responsibility. The theatre must have actors with a code of ethics and a sense of discipline, just as it must have actors with talent who have mastered their professional technique. Stanislavski said, "Every interference with collective work and every attempt to strive for personal profit or success hurts the whole; it is a violation of the personal and artistic ethic of an artist. Creativity is possible only in the right atmosphere."

Human emotions have countless nuances. When you receive the news of your father's death, one kind of sad emotion arises; when you lose ten dollars in the back seat of a cab, there is a different kind of sad emotion. An actor trained in the Stanislavski final technique can stir precisely the right emotion for a particular moment in the life of a character. To acquire the degree of conscious control required to stir such subtle reactions the System must be assimilated. You will achieve it through training and constant practice.

The Stanislavski System permits an actor to control consciously the apparatus of experience and of incarnation. The Method of Physical Actions, based on the psychophysical process, was considered by Stanislavski to be the result of his whole life's work and the heart of his system. It is the summary of his teachings and the means for stirring emotions, thoughts, imagination—all the psychic forces. When an actor controls psychophysical behavior in the given circumstances, he achieves concentration of his senses, thoughts, feelings, memory, and body.

Psychophysical behavior, or in Stanislavski's language, psychophysical action, is the means of an actor's expression. The character is built with typical psychological and physical behavior. To become actors you must be capable of choosing and fulfilling typical, expressive actions for your character.

Theatre is the profession of action. And a physical action is an act of human behavior that is part of a continuous, uninterrupted psychophysical process. But here I want to clarify a common confusion. Everybody talks about actions, but they sometimes confuse them with movements.

Physical movement is physical action stripped of any context or meaning. For example, if someone were to run in the street for no reason or purpose, that would be a physical movement. But, in fact, this never happens in life, and it must not happen on stage, for the circumstances dictate the action. In life there is always meaning, purpose, psychology. These must be visible on stage, too; they transform a movement into an action. Running into the street to save a baby from a house on fire, for example, is an action not a movement.

To understand the psychological process that leads to a physical action I have turned to the Greek philosopher Aristotle. According to Aristotle, when we see or hear something new, the first human reaction is astonishment. Astonishment, said Aristotle, leads us to philosophize about what we have experienced. Philosophy leads us to a decision, a decision produces a gesture that expresses our psychophysical state. And the result of all this is a physical action. The process he describes is one we carry on without interruption all the time in our daily life, and it is the process we must recreate on stage.

The training of your psychological instrument alone is not sufficient. You must take body movement, speech, and Shakespeare classes in addition to acting technique. There are two inseparable parts in the training and formation of an actor. One is the preparation of an actor's apparatus: his body, voice, speech, his powers of observation and imagination, his constant control over the "feeling of truth," his spiritual involvement. This is where an actor's training begins, and I'd better tell you right away that it never stops. You must continue to practice through your entire life. The other part of the training is the actor's education—the education of the future artist who must create. It is important to develop yourself personally—your culture, your needs, your will to learn, and your artistic point of view.

■ ■ ■

Let us now turn to the exercises. Please come on stage. Stand in a circle. Check your posture: heels together, toes a little apart. Keep your knees stretched and your diaphragm and stomach pulled in and your voice will benefit as well. Buttocks in, shoulders down and back, chest out. Feel an uplift. Look straight forward and relax your neck. Check tension in your fingers.

Stand behind one another. You will all be walking, but each of you will walk within the situation that you have built. So each of you must first have your own important objective; build an imaginary situation in which you walk. Think of why you are walking and where you are walking.

Now, before you begin, take time to wonder whether you are doing the right thing. Is your destination correct? Now, I don't want abstract intellectual wondering. To stir the feeling of wonder you must actually move a muscle in your torso which is attached to that feeling of wonder. That's right. Even as some of you are wondering whether there can be such a muscle, there you are using it! Very good! All mental processes are connected through the paths of nerves with the muscles that are near our spines. Try to find the muscle that is connected to your feeling of wonder

Now evaluate. How do you feel about it? You cannot feel at will, but if you locate the muscle attached to that feeling, you will stir the feeling. Experiment; try to find this muscle. Do not stop moving the muscles. And now make a decision. All must be done in the situation which you have built. When we are making a decision, we argue with ourselves. Move the muscles to stir that mental process and to express it. And now, you must make an expressive gesture that summarizes your wondering, evaluating, and the decision. Each step must flow into the other; each step must stimulate the next. Once you have made an expressive gesture, complete your physical action. Walk. Yes, that's right.

Now let us build a situation in which you sit down. First comes the event. It must be an important event. Give it a noun name. Next comes the objective, and it must be very important. Think of the circumstances in which you are sitting. For instance, are you at a reception at the White House? Or are you in the waiting room of a doctor? Are you tired or bored? Please, know the objective and circumstances. Think of the emotion you are supposed to experience. When you know which emotion it is, think of an analogous emotion in your own life. Don't try to push this emotion, just know what emotion you must go through. Take your time to build it. Good. Now, stand four steps from your chairs.

Once you know the given circumstances and have remembered an emotion analogous to the one the situation requires, you must go through all the steps of a psychophysical action. Again you first wonder about what you are going to do. (Wondering is my word for what Aristotle called "astonishment.") Next you must evaluate (what Aristotle called "philosophizing"). After evaluating, you will come to a decision, make a gesture expressing your state of mind, and only then may you carry out the physical action you intend: in this case, sitting down. But you must not try to carry out these steps in your mind alone; you must use the muscles of your body to stimulate each step in turn.

See your spine in your mind's eye. There are muscles at each side of the spine. Locate the muscle that is connected with your wondering. Don't keep your hands in your pockets. Keep your hands free. Hands are important, but they are for important gestures. Do not move your shoulders or your neck. Only the muscles. It is tremendously difficult when there is nothing in your mind to stimulate the muscles. But you can learn it. And you will control it. Experiment. Move all the muscles.

You must achieve the state of "wonder" and proceed without interruption to evaluating. Do not stop moving your muscles. Consciously reach the muscle that has triggered your evaluation, your feeling, and thoughts. Without any interruption try to locate the muscle around your spine to stir your decision.

If your muscles do not move it means that there is nothing in your mind. And now make an expressive gesture. It must be meaningful; it must express your psychophysical state. Now go to your chairs. Start and stop with another gesture. It does not have to be big but it must be expressive. Now right after that gesture sit down. This is how the action "to sit on a chair" is fulfilled in life and on stage.

Now, run around relaxing your body, your hands. When I clap my hands, stop in any position. Start running, go on, go on.

(*Mrs. Moore claps her hands.*)

Freeze. Do not change your poses. Build an imaginary situation. What is your objective? Why did you stop in such a strange way? Where are you? Build the circumstances. Think of the emotion you should experience and remember an analogous emotion in your own life. When you are ready, begin to wonder. Move your muscles, try to reach the muscle attached to your sense of wonder. Continue, continue, and begin to evaluate. Do you like what is happening or are you afraid? Without the slightest interruption, make a decision. When we make a decision we argue with ourselves. Find the muscle that will trigger this state in your mind. Make a gesture. And now from your pose, complete your original intention at the point that I stopped you. You have now fulfilled your physical ation. It's not just movement anymore, is it?

Let's do a vocal exercise. Your posture is the same as in the walking exercise. Pull your diaphragm in and feel an uplift. If you have one leg in front, you may bend its knee, but the weight of your body should be on the leg behind with a straight knee.

Inhale, don't let your diaphragm out. It must be always in or the air you inhale loses support. When inhaling, the ribs dilate. As soon as you inhale start the sound "mi." Begin the sound on your teeth and start it at once or you will lose your breath. Begin the sound "mi" and turn it into "la." Continue. Thank you.

Now divide into two groups and face one another. One group accuses the other, and the other group defends itself. Know your objective. Build the circumstances, know why you are accusing and why you are defending yourselves. Do it with the sound "mi." All right. But before accusing or defending yourself, wonder, for instance, how this could happen. Stir this sense of wonder with the muscles of your torso. Now, stir the evaluation of your feeling with the muscles of your torso, then make a decision and an expressive gesture. Only then can you accuse or defend yourself, and it will be a verbal action. Any action, verbal or physical, is preceded and ends with a meaningful gesture.

Let us proceed with a silent improvisation. Would someone please open the door?

(*John opens the door.*)*

Why did you open it?

John: Because you asked me to.

S.M.: Right. You opened the door in a certain situation. In life whatever we do always takes place in certain

---

*To avoid repetition, in these pages exercises will be tried by just a few students. In class, however, *every* student performs *every* exercise.

circumstances. In life when you open a door you know where it happens and why you do it. With this first improvisation you become aware of what you do in life. On stage, the author provides the circumstances as well as the other characters and the play's whole world. But here in class you must build the circumstances yourselves.

Imagine another situation in which you open a door. Unless you build the circumstances, your action will be a mechanical cliché. Build the imaginary circumstances in your mind. Think. Take out your notebooks and write down the order in which an improvisation must be built. First comes the event. Give a noun name to the event. Then comes your objective. Then the circumstances in which this event is taking place. Write down the emotion that must be stirred. Remember an analogous emotion that you experienced in life, but do not try to experience it. The situation does not have to be the same, only the emotion. Write down the actions that you must fulfill in order to achieve your objective. It is the event, your objective, and the circumstances that will dictate your actions.

Do not attempt to be anyone but yourself in improvisations. However, you may be in different circumstances: a student, a doctor, a teacher. Know where and why you do what you do. Opening a door is different in a hospital, in an office, or on a train. Know when it happens, too, because it is different during the day and at night. While building the circumstances you are developing your imagination and your concentration on inner objects. Your imagination will develop and the circumstances you build will become richer, and your actions more truthful.

Whatever you do on stage must be clear to your audience. When you speak you must be heard and understood; when you open the door, the audience must understand why, where, and when it is happening. Before you open the door, you must take in the situation. You must wonder, for instance, who could possibly call on you at this late hour. Move muscles around your spine to find the one that will stir this mental activity. Now evaluate and come to a decision. All this must be made clear in the gestures you make before and after opening the door. Remember that you are on stage to make everything that happens clear to those who come to the theatre.

Every improvisation must have a beginning, a development, and an end. Whenever you begin doing something in life you always change what you were doing before. For instance, before you open the door you might have been studying. Therefore, whenever you fulfill an action you are overcoming an obstacle. If you were doing important work and heard a knock at the door, you would probably take a little time to wonder, to evaluate what was happening and put aside your book before opening it. You will find the right actions if you ask yourself "What would I do in life IF I had to open the door in the circumstances that I have built here?" This IF, which Stanislavski called the "magic if," is truly miraculous. Honestly answer the question "What would I do IF?" And behave the way you would in life.

(*Kathy attempts the improvisation.*)

S.M.: Did you know where this happened, Kathy?

Kathy: Yes.

S.M.: Good, but the audience must know it, too. Your behavior must project your circumstances.

Before actually starting the improvisation try to bring yourself into the psychophysical state in the circumstances you have built. Your mind and body must be as involved as they are in life. Wonder in the situation you have built by locating the muscle attached to this mental activity. Try to reach another muscle connected to the evaluation of what happened. Don't stop moving your muscles. Now make a decision, argue with yourself. Go on, experiment with the muscles; and now make an expressive gesture. It should express the state you have achieved. Try hard. The gesture must express what you feel but do not say. It does not have to be big. It depends on the situation you have built. Gestures of the body often project the subtext, the ultimate meaning of the drama.

Now let us "close the door." Concentrate and build the circumstances: why you close the door, where you close it, and so on. *How* you do it is very important, but do not think about it until you know your objective and the circumstances. Otherwise you will limit your imagination. You will do it in different ways in different circumstances; therefore build them first and the situation will suggest how to do it.

(*The students perform the improvisation.*)

S.M.: Some of you tried to make faces to indicate something. Please do not do this. Indicating is wrong. Know your objective. Overcome at least one obstacle on your way toward it. And remember that every physical action must be needed; it must be necessary to overcome the obstacles you confront.

Tom, why did you close the door? I did not understand it.

Tom: Because I didn't want to let the dog out.

S.M.: Is this the outside door?

Tom: Yes, and there is a storm going on.

S.M.: You know what is going on outside, and you are satisfied with this knowledge. You do not care that the people who have come to see you and paid good money for their seats have no idea about either the dog inside, the storm outside or what you were doing on stage.

Tom: I thought you didn't want us to indicate.

S.M.: And you are right. An indication is only a mechanical movement. When Kathy took her pill, this could have been an obvious way to indicate that she was leaving a doctor's office, but she convinced us that she had to take it. You did not fulfill a psychophysical action that happens in definite circumstances and is directed toward a definite purpose.

Of course, in a production there would be a real dog, and that part of it would be easier. But there will be other things to project that will be more difficult than the presence of a dog. These are only the first steps to achieve the greatest expressiveness and lifelike behavior on stage. If you cannot project something it does not belong on stage. There is no art if it does not reach the audience.

Let's proceed to the next improvisation. Here is an antique. Yes, a very precious object. Looking at this dirty bottle, you do not have to try to believe it is valuable. All you have to do is treat it as if it were. If you find and perform truthful actions, treat it as an antique and succeed in convincing us that it is one, you will begin to believe it yourself because you are doing it as you would in life. Before thinking of how to do it, please build the imaginary circumstances: why you handle it, where, when, and so on.

(*Improvisation by Chris.*)

S.M.: Please, Chris, do not stop an improvisation until I stop you. It was not clear to me what kind of object it was, and I was hoping that you would improve and find more expressive adaptations. What you did, you could do with a bottle of Scotch.

Chris: It was probably because I put it into the closet. I am trying to project that I am always afraid to leave my antiques lying around on tables, and this one is especially valuable to me.

S.M.: How on earth could we have known all that? You did not take it in, did not evaluate.

Chris: I knew very well what I was doing.

S.M.: But it is not enough that you knew it. No matter how interesting your ideas are, they have no value if you do not find the form that expresses them. Go on. Yes, you, Sharon.

(*Improvisation by Sharon.*)

You did too many things—combed your hair, tied your shoe, put on lipstick. What did all this have to do with handling an antique? Any action that does not project what you must project is harmful. It distracts those who watch you from what is essential. What we saw you doing seemed to come out of the blue, and you could have been doing it in different circumstances.

Sharon: I agree with you. Did you at least know that I was in an antique shop?

S.M.: Yes.

(*Ruth performs the improvisation.*)

Well, Ruth, you treated the bottle very carefully—I think too carefully. It looked as if you were handling a baby. In such cases Stanislavski used to say, "Cut ninety-five percent." You should always watch for what he called "the measure of truth."

Do you all have the paperback copy of *The Three Sisters* that I asked you to buy? Did you read the play? How many times? Once is not enough. You will have to read it many times in order to understand what Chekhov wanted to say. We will discuss the play later, after you read it again.

■ Class Two

SONIA MOORE: Please come on stage, and we will perform an exercise called "disobeying hands." It will warm you up. Your right arm goes forward. Think of what you are doing with your arm stretched like that. Think of why you are doing it, and where. Adjust your body so that it expresses what you do. Move the muscles around your spine to stir wonder and the rest of the steps in the psychophysical process. Another gesture. Now raise your arm. Think of what you are doing, and express it with your body. Anyone entering this room should understand what you are doing without hearing any words. Now move your arm to the side and build the situation in your mind and adjust your body; go through all the psychophysical steps.

Now do the same thing but use both arms, with the left lagging one movement behind the right. When the right arm goes up, the left goes forward; when the right goes to the side, the left goes up; right goes down, left to the side; and so on. For each position evoke an image of what you are doing and make sure your body expresses it. And when you stand still continue moving the muscles around your spine, wondering about what you are doing, evaluating, deciding, and gesturing before and after you move your arms. Good. Now put your arms down.

Some of you have expressed legitimate confusion

about what I mean when I say move the muscles in your torso in order to create an appropriate emotional state. This does not surprise me. What I want you to do is very difficult. It took Stanislavski his entire career to discover it.

Because our psychological life and our physical existence are connected to one another, in life our bodies express our feelings naturally, instinctively. So it seemed only natural to Stanislavski that when we recreate a character's emotional life on stage, we must recreate this process, and try to achieve an emotional state in our mind that our bodies could then express. This is what Stanislavski did in his early experiments. He had his actors push emotions in ways that were not healthy and brought them to a point of hysteria.

But late in his studies Stanislavski had an inspiration based on the simplest of facts: that because the mind and the body influence each other, the influence can flow in both directions. This is the basis of the Method of Physical Actions: that we can use our muscles to reach feelings rather than rely on feelings to stimulate our muscles. In particular, there are muscles in the torso, around the spine, attached to mental processes that, when reached will bring you into the correct psychological state in your character's situation. Does this mean that you must jump and shrug every time you wish to achieve and project a psychophysical state? No. But you must learn to find and touch these muscles if you are to achieve psychophysical coordination and spontaneity on stage.

Now we will perform an improvisation: "reading at home." Before you do the improvisation you must first build the imaginary situation. Do you have notebooks?

Write these things down. You must know the event and your objective: Are you reading in preparation for an exam? An audition? Know your circumstances. Have in mind the people you know who might be involved in this objective, such as your teacher or casting director. What are you reading and when? Reading at night may be different from reading during the day. Write these things down; they must be concrete. Know what emotion you must stir. Furnish the room with the tables and chairs we have, and please use props, but only if they will help you. The props are in the closet.

Are you ready, Dan? Go on.

(*Dan sits in a chair and reads.*)

How are we to know that you were in your own room and not in the lobby of a hotel? You must select a chain of logical actions to project your objective and the circumstances that you have built. Everything you do on stage must be clear to the audience. A play lasts about two and a half hours usually, and in that time you must express the life of the character and the meaning of the whole play. To do it in that time, you must find the most expressive actions and discard those that do not help. During your improvisation, we had no idea that you were at home, whether you were reading for pleasure or because you had to, and so on. You must know your objective.

Dan: Something is distracting me, and I don't feel like reading. Anyway, the book is too long.

S.M.: Well, that is interesting, but you are the only one who knows it. You are speaking of obstacles. You must have an important objective for your reading and project overcoming the obstacles to it. Every action must project "reading at home."

Now, Joan.

(*Joan performs the improvisation.*)

That was good. You can see how simple, expressive actions can project what you want to project. She was so engrossed in her book that she carried it to the refrigerator when she went for something to eat. Her objective not to waste a minute was clear.

Now we are going to "read in the library." Do not go on stage until you have built the circumstances.

(*Robert performs the improvisation.*)

S.M.: What disturbs me is that you moved the table. Would you move it in a library?

Robert: No. I wouldn't.

S.M.: Otherwise it was good, and I am satisfied. When you come to a more advanced stage of actual work on a role, you will realize how difficult it is to select the right actions. That is why you are learning it in these improvisations.

(*Ruth does the improvisation.*)

What were you writing?

Ruth: Some lines from a poem, but I was distracted by people in the library.

S.M.: Yes, you made it clear that there were people around you. But looking around at people like that can also be done in a café. You did not take in people, did not evaluate, did not make a decision. Also you held your book in your lap, and it seems to me that people in a library keep their books on the table.

All of you, please, do not be upset when I criticize you. I do not expect you to do it right. I am trying to put you on the right road. In addition to training your instrument, you must master the choice of actions, that is, the choice of appropriate behavior. And this takes longer than training your instrument. So you must start learning it now, in these simple improvisations. Remember, the actions you choose will be artistic only if they are needed; if they are vital to the situation.

Now let us turn to *The Three Sisters*. Did you all have a chance to read it again? If you did not you should do so, and if you did you should read it yet another time. Read it again and again.

In *The Three Sisters*, Chekhov is writing about the longing for a better life. His characters are subtle, well-mannered people who love each other but also have isolated inner worlds of their own Their tragedy is that they submit to evil without fighting it. They are tortured by boredom, anguish, monotony, but they are unable to do anything. Moscow is the symbol of their faraway ideals, which will never be realized, and Natasha and Protopopov are symbols of vulgarity. Trivialities invade people's lives; it is a dangerous force, and Chekhov is warning us against it.

I am describing the superobjective of the play. "Superobjective" is Stanislavski's term for the intent of the play; what the author wanted to say. The superobjective runs throughout the play. When we work on scenes from *The Three Sisters*, or any other play, we will often talk about objectives within the scene; but these are situation objectives, which either advance the play toward the superobjective or block its progress in that direction. When actors choose situation objectives they must never forget the superobjective.

The first act takes place on Irina's saint's day. In old Russia, as in many parts of Europe, one's saint's day was as important as a birthday. In this scene it is spring, with singing birds, flowers, gaiety.

When we study the play, we give a noun name to every event or episode. Let us call this episode that begins the play "celebration." This means that all the performers in this episode must project "celebration." The actions will be different for everyone. For instance, Olga insists that everything is wonderful, Irina is building happy plans for the future, and Masha is trying to block out her troubles so as not to spoil Irina's saint's day. Let us read Olga's first speech, which begins the play.

> **OLGA:** Father died exactly a year ago, on this very day, the fifth of May—your saint's day, Irina. It was so cold, and snow was falling. It seemed to me that I would never live through it, and you were lying unconscious as if you were dead. And now a year later we can talk of it easily, you are already wearing a white dress, your face glows. (*A clock strikes twelve.*) And the clock was striking then, too. (*Pause*) It comes back to me that when Father was carried away, music was playing and at the cemetery they fired a salute. He was a general, in command of a brigade, and yet there were only a few people. But it was raining then. Heavy rain, and snowing.

S.M.: One of the first steps in building a character is to create images in your mind that correspond to those of the character. If you are playing Olga, when you say "Father died . . ." you must have an image in your mind of a man who means to you what Olga's father means to her. He does not have to be your own father, but he should be a real person. Dig deep into your memory and bring out people, events, and places that you really know.

I will demonstrate how these images appear in your mind in real life. Will you all think of someone you met today who impressed you in some way? All right, Robert. Who was it—a man? A woman?

Robert: It was a taxi driver.

S.M.: Describe his clothes.

Robert: His jacket was brown and pretty dirty, and he also wore dark glasses.

S.M.: How old was he?

Robert: Oh, about fifty-five.

S.M.: Do you think he is married?

Robert: . . Yes.

S.M.: Is he a good husband?

Robert: I think so . . . and I think he is a good father.

S.M.: Are you aware that as you spoke you saw in your mind the man and everything you said about him? You were wondering, evaluating, and deciding before every answer and your gestures continued expressing these mental processes after your answers. Robert, do you think he is a good-natured man?

Robert: I think he is, but he wasn't today because he told me that he had worked twelve hours, and this would not put anyone in a good humor. He said he loves to drive and would like to have a day off and drive out to Long Island. So I figured he loves his work.

S.M.: Do you all realize that you had mental images for what Robert said, and your bodies expressed your feeling? Now, Joan, tell us about someone you met today.

Joan: I don't remember anyone.

S.M.: Make an effort and you will.

Joan: Oh, I remember a woman I saw in a restaurant with a red hat and a green dress. She looked like Christmas. That's all I can remember.

S.M.: Are you aware that when you describe it, you see it? When poor actors read their lines, they rush over them, seeing nothing. In life our images are spontaneous, and we take them for granted, but on stage you must form them consciously. You must learn to stir the images you have chosen with your muscles, to describe them, and to express your feeling about them through gestures during pauses in your lines so vividly that your fellow actors see them, too, and so that you also stir the images and associations of the audience. When you as Olga say "On the fifth of May—your saint's day, Irina," you must have your own real images of a party and people that are right for Olga. When you say "It was cold and snowing," you must see New York or any other place that means to you what this town means to Olga. Do not try to see Moscow, for it does not mean a thing to you. You must see images in your mind; the muscles of your body must stir them; and your gestures must express your attitude to them before you speak and when you stop speaking. Otherwise your words will be dead sounds.

Before you work on images, you must read the play many times and write a biography of the character you will be portraying. While you read the play, note all the hints about your character, both from what you say and from what others say about you. Write down what you think of your character. When you know him or her well, you will be ready to begin building the character's spiritual life.

To portray a character you also must be able to make use of the *inner monologue*. Irina does not have any lines during Olga's speech at the beginning of *The Three Sisters*, but she must be thinking continuously. This thinking is the inner monologue. It is the continuation of the character's life during silences. It occurs when another character is speaking, for example, or when you are taking a pause. The psychophysical steps we have talked about—wondering, evaluating, making decisions—make up the inner monologue; the muscles stimulate the emotions, thoughts, and images a character experiences when he or she is silent. In the past I have told students to write down their inner monologue, but I no longer believe you should do this. If, when you are silent, you move the muscles that stir the psychophysical steps, you will have created an inner monologue. But you must not think that any inner monologue will do; if you are to portray the character conceived by the author, you must choose images, thoughts, and emotions that are appropriate for the character. We will work on this in exercises, improvisations, and in your scenes from the play.

Pat, Joan, and Debbi, you will work on the role of Irina. In this scene Irina is building dream castles in her mind. Your thoughts and images must be your own, which would be right for Irina. They must mean to you what Irina's thoughts and images mean to her. Remember that at this point Irina is still hopeful and thinks that life can be wonderful.

I would like Maria and Kathy to work on Olga. Ruth and Sharon, you will work on Masha, and if you read the play you will know that Masha does not say a word at the beginning. Therefore you, too, must have continuous thoughts during the scene. You will learn that those actors who do not say a word occupy as important a place on stage as those who speak—sometimes even more important. Life does not stop when we are silent. Thoughts flash through our minds all the time.

Images and inner monologue are essential steps toward building the character. They are part of the *second plan*—this was Nemirovich-Danchenko's term. The existence of a character on stage is only a small part of his whole life; the second plan includes his life before the play and after it. Like Stanislavski, Nemirovich-

Danchenko believed that the audience must be made aware of the whole inner life of the character, his entire destiny, while he is on stage.

If you do not use images and inner monologue, you will only be another prop. Actors who do not use them on stage, Stanislavski said, look like prematurely born people. But to be able to do this, you must know and understand the play. You must understand the meaning Chekhov wants to project.

Later in the first act, Irina says, "Masha is in a bad mood today." *You* must know why you as Masha are in a bad mood. Masha is refined, talented, and bored. She is a happy person; she loves life; she may be the only one here who faces life, who knows that life is difficult and still loves it. She has more courage than her sisters, but today she wants to leave her sister's party. Why? Think of thoughts that would be right for you as Masha, or you as Irina, and try to find muscles around your spine that will turn on these thoughts.

I think that Chris and Robert should work on the role of Andrei. Tom, Dan, John, and Mat work on Baron Tusenbach and Soliony. We shall work on the beginning of the first act. The scene starts with Olga's speech and ends with Baron Tusenbach's entrance. We will also work on the scene with Andrei and Ferapont in Act Two. Read the play many times, and give it more thought. Then write biographies of your characters. Search for analogous emotions, images of people, places, and events in your own life that would be right for the moment when you say your character's lines. And at the same time find muscles around your spine that you can move to stir these mental processes.

■ Class Three

SONIA MOORE: Please put your chairs in a circle and sit down. Now think: what are you doing sitting in the circle? Know your objective. Build the circumstances. As you are sitting, wonder about why you are there, evaluate your position, make a decision about what to do next, and then summarize the whole process of thought and feeling with a gesture that expresses your state of mind.

Now, without looking at each other, stand up together and turn toward your chairs. Before each movement you must wonder, evaluate, come to a decision, and make an expressive gesture. Take hold of the chairs and raise them. Why are you doing this? You must know, and your gestures must express that knowledge. Let me show you what I mean. Put the chairs down. Everyone get up on stage and walk around quickly. When I give the signal, stop and assume any pose.

Stop.

All right, Tom, why did you take that pose?

Tom: Because I thought someone was near me.

S.M.: Drop the pose. Now assume it again with that justification in mind.

And you, Kathy, why did you stop?

Kathy: Because I got some sand in my eyes.

S.M.: Take it in, evaluate. Relax and take the pose again with your justification in mind. Good. Dan, why did you stop?

Dan: There is water under my feet.

S.M.: Start walking again, and stop for that reason. Find muscles to stir the mental processes and gestures to project them. All right. Express the reason for the pose you have taken. Be sure that your movements are purposeful actions.

Let us try a more complex improvisation. There was a crime committed last night. You are all suspected of being the attacker. You come in and sit down. The victim of the attack is going to identify the guilty person. Decide whether you are guilty or innocent. Give a noun name to the event. Have an objective. The "magic if" is of great help if you use it honestly. Ask yourself "What would I do if I were innocent of this crime? Guilty of it?" Know your objective. Build the circumstances. Imagine the other people involved; use people you know. Imagine what you would do with your body—how you would hold your head, what you would do with your hands. Before each movement wonder, evaluate, come to a decision about what to do, and make a gesture expressing your state of mind. Move after the gesture, fulfill your physical action. When you finish moving, make another gesture. The gesture does not have to be big, but it must have meaning.

Now you hear a voice ordering you to rise and turn

around slowly because the victim of the attack must see you in profile. You cannot see this person. With a gesture, express your attitude to that order. You hear now an order to sit down again. Respond, sit, and project to us with one more gesture your response to the whole experience.

Let us try one more improvisation. The girls have discovered that they have lost a piece of jewelry, and the men have lost their wallets. Know your objectives. Build the circumstances. Know when you discovered the loss; where; what kind of jewelry it was, who gave it to you, whether it was insured, or how much money was in the wallet, and so on. It may be a family heirloom or a present from your fiancé. Your objective and the circumstances will determine your actions. I want this to be an important loss for you. Make an effort and remember an analogous emotion in your life when something unpleasant happened to you.

The circumstances do not have to be the same as they were in life, but the emotion that you went through must be analogous. Think what you did or would do in such a case if it happened in real life. Do not push your emotions. Wonder, evaluate, and make your decisions. The right muscles will stir the right emotions. Do not try to "act" or to amuse us.

(*Dan performs the improvisation.*)

This should be important to you! You seem to be imitating someone with your own "I don't care" style. I am afraid that if you follow that style you will not be interested in building characters either, and will always play your own passive self—and this is not even yourself, but your mannerisms, your own image of yourself.

(*Improvisation by Tom.*)

That was pretty good, but your tempo-rhythm did not change when you realized that you had lost your wallet.

Tom: What do you mean by tempo-rhythm?

S.M.: Tempo-rhythm is Stanislavski's term for the speed and intensity of your actions. All of your actions were in the same tempo-rhythm, and that is why they weren't truthful. In life any little change of circumstance stirs a different tempo-rhythm. Watch for this in your own life; you will see how often the rhythm of your actions changes as your objective and circumstances change.

Stanislavski said, "If you learn to think and to fulfill actions, and in addition you have control of your tempo-rhythms, you're in the driver's seat." Rhythm expresses inner experience, and control over it is one of the conditions for mastering the inner technique. Overcoming obstacles on the way to your objective should be of tremendous help in changing the tempo-rhythm.

I do not mean that after discovering the loss you must become frantic. You might even stop entirely to wonder and evaluate what has happened. In life we do not have to think about the change of tempo; it takes care of itself. But when you work on roles, you must be aware of it as an essential element of truthful action. Tempo-rhythm is essential for uniting the psychological and the physical in an action. It discloses the depth of human experience. It may vary while you are talking; be aware of this, too. I would like all of you to think up at home some theme on the change of tempo-rhythm. Create obstacles and think of ways to overcome them.

Kathy: Would the tempo-rhythm change depending on the value of the object that was lost?

S.M.: Of course. Can you imagine what would happen if you lost a thousand dollars that might not even belong to you? Or let us say you lost an earring that you bought at a five-and-ten. These are all different circumstances. Once you know the circumstances you must decide what actions are necessary, then carry them out. In this case you might decide to look in your pocket or a bureau; you might decide to call an insurance broker or the police. In life we constantly make decisions to do something or to refrain from doing something. These decisions will be expressed by your body with gestures.

You are training your instrument and taking control of it in order to be able to build the inner spiritual world of another human being with your own resources. You will build a new person who has different thoughts, different images, different emotions—a completely different inner world from your own. But you will start with yourself. An actor creates a work of art with himself; he is his own instrument. A pianist has the piano, a painter the paint: but the actor has only his own organic nature and his body. He is the creator and the creation all at once. And so I tell you: if you do not connect the psychological and the physical behavior, you will not become actors—not even if you study for twenty years.

It is now time to tell you more about the *emotional memory*, a most important attribute of the actor's art. Past emotions, and every adult person has gone through a great deal of emotions, leave a trace on our central nervous system and make the nerves that participate more sensitive. To experience a true emotion on stage, an actor must stir in his emotional memory the imprint of an analogous emotion. Now you see why, in exercises and improvisations, I have been asking you to remember an "analogous emotion!"

We have all experienced different feelings of love, hate, suffering, rejoicing, etc. These feelings may have been caused by different reasons—we may suffer a headache, or because a friend has passed away—but something is common to the experience; that is why in both cases we call the emotion "suffering." The emotional memory, in addition to retaining the imprints of emotions, also synthesizes emotions of related but different natures. If we have experienced "suffering" many times, even for different reasons, the common element in the emotion will have left a deep imprint on our memory.

⌐The quality of an actor's performance depends upon the sincerity of his emotions. The actor must live true emotions, but true stage emotions. Stanislavski called these "repeated emotions" and distinguished them from the "primary emotions" we experience in life. Through rehearsals, experiments, and the use of the muscle connected to the needed emotion, an actor will develop a conditioned reflex in which the repeated emotion is stirred on stage. Though absolutely sincere, this emotion does not absorb the actor completely; he never forgets that he is performing on stage. If the actor is honest, he will admit that an authentic emotion of suffering while performing gave him true joy.

As you know, in the early stages of the System actors were forcing their emotions. Stanislavski realized that forcing emotions brought actors to inner hysteria, and this was detrimental to the actor's health and to art. With the Method of Physical Actions Stanislavski found the means to achieve the creative spontaneous state. You have been studying this means. To relive the emotion stored in an actor's emotional memory, he must be capable of selecting a physical action that is purposeful, indispensable, muscular, and true to the given circumstances. It must have a clear objective, as I have stressed. To stir an emotion, you must find and move the muscle connected to it. Moreover, when you find that muscle, you will find the means to restir the emotion every time you perform.

To enrich the reservoir of your emotional memory, you must observe the outside world—an inexhaustible source. You must visit museums, see paintings, study sculpture, listen to music, and watch people. Listening to music, observing nature, and admiring works of art enrich your impressions and help you learn more about yourself. You will be able to see what the artist who created a work of art wanted to express. You will learn to register what others do not notice, and express it for them on stage. You will have in your memory a reserve of images that you will be able to use as an artist uses sketches. There is life around us everywhere, and it provides a limitless treasury for observation. Do not limit your observations to yourself. "Store" what you see, and someday you may use it for building a character.

And now to *The Three Sisters*.

Did you read the play again? Good. Do you think you

know what Chekhov wanted to say with this play? Keep in mind that whatever you do in your roles must help to disclose the superobjective. I want you to think of all the conflicts in the play. Bringing out the conflicts will reveal the themes of the play.

Every detail must contribute to the atmosphere on stage. When you choose your images and know what should be on your mind, you must be certain that this helps to project that these lovely, noble people cannot fight the triviality they are caught in. To build a character means to establish his relationship with the surrounding world, his attitude toward every fact and event.

Kathy: Mrs. Moore, I cannot understand these people. They seem so weak and ineffective.

S.M.: Yes, they are weak. Through them Chekhov discloses what was in the hearts of all the Russian intelligentsia: their dream of a better future. Chekhov tells us about a life without purpose, the dull, uneventful days of people whose minds, as time passes, are gradually invaded by the dangerous force of triviality. He shows how this threatening force penetrates people, kills their dreams and sometimes their serious ambitions. Anguish and boredom torture Chekhov's characters. He wanted to inspire people to search for a better future, which can be achieved only through hard work. He demonstrates two antagonistic forces—on one hand the subtle feelings of good people, their beautiful souls, their inner search for a road to happiness, and on the other hand the degrading force of vulgarity.

In the first act it is springtime; there are singing birds,

flowers, sunshine. The arrival of Vershinin puts everyone into a wonderful mood. Masha, who had been bored, suffering from the lack of real people around her, revives. Vershinin, the dreamer who savors his philosophizing, is unable to stop it even when it embarrasses him. Though his life is distorted, Vershinin still wants to dream of what it could be. He is accepted with joy at this house, and he frequents it as if it were his own. Tusenbach, the passionate dreamer, is overwhelmed with his love for Irina. This wonderful man spreads goodness around him. He is liked by everybody and likes everyone. Even in Soliony, the gloomy officer, he does not find any great faults.

Act One is happy. It is the end of a year of mourning for the dead father. Irina decides to go to work and dreams about it. Tusenbach now can speak of love to Irina. Masha and Vershinin meet; Andrei proposes to Natasha. And Olga does not have her usual headache.

Now. Have you all written biographies of the characters you will be working on? I do not want to rush you, but please, do it for the next class.

Let us try the first scene of the play with Kathy, Joan, and Ruth. On the stage is the living room of the Prosorov family. It is around noon on a cheerful spring day. Irina is full of hope; Olga does not permit herself to be sad; only Masha is in a bad mood. All think of your physical state. Masha is trying to concentrate on the book, but she cannot. She is haunted by a line from a poem. Irina is immersed in happy thoughts, and she does not hear Olga.

Our stage is very small, and it is difficult not to hear, but you will have to stir in your mind such a strong and exciting inner monologue that it will seem natural that you do not hear anything. Joan, you must choose images of people you know who would be right for Irina. Concentrate on the muscles around your spine; they must stir images and thoughts. Do not smile; when you achieve lifelike behavior, your eyes will radiate your happy thoughts.

Olga has been correcting her school papers. Bring a few sheets of paper and a pencil, Kathy. What would you do if you were correcting papers as Olga?

Kathy: I would be sitting.

S.M.: All right, you think you would be sitting. Olga is in a hurry because they are expecting guests for dinner to celebrate Irina's saint's day, and she must supervise the servants. But the next day is a school day, she is a teacher, and she must finish correcting papers. The clock strikes and it brings back memories of what happened last year at the same time. Then Olga speaks. Kathy, begin.

> **Kathy**: Father died exactly a year ago, on this very day, the fifth of May—

S.M.: Kathy, stop. Olga's objective is to encourage her sisters, and her action is to compare this day with the same day last year. It is not mourning; although the pain is still there, Olga is determined to build a new, better life.

To convey this, you must first of all be conscious of your objective and circumstances. You must think of these at home. You must know the girls whose papers you are correcting, or two of them at least. And before saying your lines—I mean, while the clock is striking—you must wonder in this situation, evaluate it, come to a decision, make a gesture. Only then can you speak. Try again.

Kathy: Father died exactly a year ago, on this very day—

S.M.: No, Kathy, you are rushing. And you are rushing because you evidently do not see anything. Words without images are dead. Before you speak you must move the muscles that will stir your thoughts, feelings, and images. A psychophysical action begins with the inner monologue—wondering, evaluating, and making decisions and a gesture expressing your psychophysical state. The process is stirred by the muscles in your torso. The action of correcting the papers must begin with this psychophysical process. It ends with another gesture. Only then will you be carrying out an action and not a mechanical movement. Only when you move the right muscles will your intonations be right, and always fresh. Images, thoughts, feelings, expressive gestures, physical actions, and words must be one uninterrupted process on stage, but I do not expect you to be ready for that now.

And do not put down the pencil when you hear the clock striking. Olga does not know that she is going to make a long speech. What would you as Olga be thinking about?

Kathy: I don't know. I didn't have time to read the play again.

S.M.: Of course, if you have read it only once, you cannot know very much about what is going through Olga's mind. I thought you had worked at home. This is not the way to build a character. But try it one more time; let us see what you can do.

Kathy: Father died exactly a year ago . . .

■ CLASS FOUR

SONIA MOORE: Now, Dan, please go on stage. Raise your right arm, squat down, and then put your hand over your eyes. Justify and connect these three movements.

Dan: I am hailing a cab; I am squatting in a dance.

S.M.: What does a cab have to do with the dance? I told you to justify and connect; the three movements must make sense together.

Dan: Oh. I hail a taxicab; I squat down to pick up a nickel I dropped; and something went into my eye.

S.M.: Very good. Next, Kathy, please come on stage. Put your hands on your hips, look up, and then bend down.

Kathy: I am thinking . . . I can't think of anything.

S.M.: Yes, you can. Make an effort.

Kathy: I have to clean this room and I don't like doing it. I put my hands on my hips, look up at the dirt everywhere, and then down at the dirt on the floor.

S.M.: Yes, but we did not see wondering, evaluating, deciding. Do it again. That is better. Now, Sharon. Touch your hair, bend down and cross your arms, justify, and connect.
(*Sharon pantomimes.*)
What was that?

Sharon: It has to do with a song. It was a feeling.

S.M.: You should justfy the movements I gave you and make them psychophysical actions. Every movement becomes an action when it has an objective, is performed in definite circumstances, and has psychology. In the Stanislavski System, what is called an *action* is an act of human behavior. When you fulfill an act of human behavior you will stir feelings.

Sharon: I lost a bobby pin. I bent down to pick it up, and I don't see it.

S.M.: Good. This exercise certainly helps to develop your imagination, which must be quick and rich because you will have to be able to find actions that are interesting in addition to being truthful and logical.

Robert: Did Stanislavski use all these exercises?

S.M.: Some, but many were created by Ivan E. Koch, who wrote a book on stage movement, and some were invented here at the school. Next we are going to hide.

John: All together?

S.M.: No, each in turn. Do not think of how you will perform it before you have a clear picture of the circumstances in your mind. Different circumstances will make you hide in very different ways. It must be obvious to you that hiding from children in a game is different than hiding from a gangster who is following you. If you think of how to hide before you build the circumstances you limit your imagination, and your hiding will be a cliché. But after you know why, when, where, and so on, you must think of *how*—the adaptation or the ways to perform in an expressive way. An action is composed of three elements: *what* you do, *why* you do it, and *how* you do it. It is with the *how* that you make your action clear to the spectators. The more imaginative *how* you are able to find the more interesting your work will be, and therefore the better actor you will be. The most important thing is to fulfill the action truthfully. Now concentrate and build the circumstances. Try to remember an analogous emotion in your life. Perhaps you were afraid of somebody. Think of people who were involved when you experienced fear. Every physical or verbal action begins and ends with an expressive gesture. Is anyone ready? All right, John. Go on.

(John performs the improvisation.)

After all I just said, I did not understand why you were hiding or where or when.

John: I had not done my homework, and I saw the teacher in the hallway, and I wanted to avoid him, so I hid behind the door.

S.M.: I did not believe you at all. You did not even hide, you just went over there. Don't you think that we should have known while you were performing the improvisation what you are telling us now? Gestures were missing. Please do it again. What did you say you were doing?

John: I was supposed to write a composition on European civilization for homework.

S.M.: That would be interesting, if you made it clear—which is not easy to do! But if you cannot project what is going on, there is no place for it on stage. John, first of all, you must project that you are not doing what you are supposed to be doing, and then suddenly you see a teacher coming. For example, couldn't you have been writing and then started playing card tricks instead or just playing around, and this is why you have to hide when the teacher comes along?
   (*Sharon performs the improvisation.*)
   Sharon, did you know the room you were hiding in?

Sharon: No. I really did not know it.

S.M.: But you went behind the screen as if you already knew it was there. That is why we do the improvisations. In life you would have had to look around before you knew that there was a screen. Whatever you do on stage must be as if you were doing it for the first time. Many little things you did failed to project why or where you were hiding. These are harmful because they clutter up what has to be projected. Only actions that help to project the situation should be used. Your objective must be clear,

and so must the obstacles on the way to it.
(*The students perform the improvisation.*)

S.M.: Please stop all improvisations that have a definite sexual quality. I shall not tolerate this kind of distortion, which has taken place in the name of Stanislavski. One of the most outrageous misrepresentations has occurred in regard to Stanislavski's "public solitude." Here is what Stanislavski said: "Public solitude is achieved when an actor is concentrated on his action and does not try to amuse his audience." This term of Stanislavski's has been transformed into a sinister "private moment."

I find this distortion offensive to the name of Stanislavski and also to human privacy. Sex is not taught or exploited in this studio. It will not teach you to become actors.

I hear about actresses who, while rehearsing a scene, become so "involved" that they tear off their blouses and perform "topless." I suggest to such actresses that they start learning the Stanislavski technique, which teaches control of an actor's behavior on stage.

I would also appreciate it if you would dispense with improvisations that take place in toilet rooms. Artists must develop their artistic taste, and such themes are in poor taste.

Now let us see the scene between Andrei and Ferapont from the second act of *The Three Sisters* with Chris as Andrei. Robert, will you please read Ferapont. We will not work on the rold of Ferapont now. He is an older man, not suitable for you to study at this stage. So, don't be either flattered or disappointed when I ignore your performance.

Andrei (Chris): Good evening, my good soul. What do you have to say?

Ferapont (Robert): The chairman has sent you a book and some kind of paper. Here.

Andrei: Thank you. Good. Why didn't you come earlier?

S.M.: (*Interrupting*) Please, Chris, do not pretend to be Andrei. It is not that easy to build a character. We will learn to do that step by step, and we have only started to work on steps toward it. And you had better eliminate that artificial laugh.

You seem to be trying to impress us with how well you read. But I want you to know why you say what you say and see the images—if you have worked on them at home. I want you to move the right muscles of your torso to stir the right inner processes and make gestures to express your inner monologue, your images, and your feelings before you speak and after you speak. Your inner experiences must reach the spectators before they hear what you say. The movement of the right muscles will stir the needed internal process, and gestures will project what words cannot project.

Only when there is a need to say the words can you expect your intonations to be right. Concentrate on your spine and muscles around it and feel the weight of your body. When we are sad our body becomes heavy. Let us repeat it. Robert, do not come in until Chris is concentrated on his wondering, evaluating, and making a decision. Chris, do you know what happened just before this moment? Do you know what is on Andrei's mind? Believe me, I do not expect much—I am only trying to put you on the right road. Natasha has left the room, and

Andrei is wondering about what has happened to him and his family. Protopopov and Natasha, as we have seen, are trivial and vulgar and Andrei is beginning to submit to Natasha without protest. Your objective is to shut out your troubles.

What kind of book has Protopopov sent you? Are you interested in it? Is it a book Protopopov promised you or did you leave it behind in the office? Or what? Chekhov is a good playwright, you know, and there must be a reason for the book. When you look at it and put it aside, we in the audience must know your attitude toward Protopopov. Then you take the paper Ferapont gives you and go into your den for a moment to sign it.

Chris: Why can't I sign it here?

S.M.: This is the living room and there is no inkstand here and remember they didn't have ballpoint pens!

> **Andrei**: Good evening, my good soul. What have you to say?
>
> **Ferapont**: The chairman has sent you a book and some kind of paper. Here.
>
> **Andrei**: Thank you. Good. Why didn't you come earlier? It's already eight.
>
> **Ferapont**: Heh?
>
> **Andrei**: I say, you came late. It's after eight already.
>
> **Ferapont**: Yes sir. I came here, it was still light, but they wouldn't let me in. The master, they say, is busy. So what. Busy is busy. I have nowhere to hurry. Heh?
>
> **Andrei**: Nothing. Tomorrow is Friday—

S.M.: I must interrupt. What is your inner monologue before you speak?

Chris: I wonder "This is how Natasha has changed our house."

S.M.: Good. Although the inner monologue does not have to be continuous—it is condensed, amorphous, broken up, and often conflicting with what we say—you must be thinking as the character. We stop thinking only when we are unconscious or dead; and the character is dead when you stop thinking as the character. To think as the character you must move your muscles. Also, when you say, "Tomorrow is Friday, I don't have to attend, but I'll go anyway, just to occupy myself," you say it in reaction to what Ferapont has said about your being busy. All you are doing is taking care of the children, because that is what Natasha wants. Did you write the biography, Chris?

Chris: Yes I did.

S.M.: You must study the character's behavior. If Andrei were a nasty man, you would have to build him differently. His behavior toward his sisters or his wife would not be the same. Let us see the scene.

> **Andrei**: Good evening, my good soul. What have you to say?
>
> **Ferapont**: The chairman has sent you a book and some kind of paper. Here.
>
> **Andrei**: Thank you. Good—

S.M.: Oh, Chris, why do you interrupt all the time? I was so happy to see that you were able to concentrate for a moment, and here you are interrupting again.

Chris: Because I don't feel anything.

S.M.: What do you want to feel?

Chris: I don't become emotional.

S.M.: The right muscle will stir the right emotion. And Chris, stop gesticulating continuously. You must study and choose your poses and gestures. Nothing can be accidental on stage except when the accidental action happens under inspiration. This is the goal of the Stanislavski System. But inspiration will not come until you have done a great deal of conscious work. Please go on and do not interrupt. And you do not have to scream at Ferapont.

Chris: But he's hard of hearing.

S.M.: This is true, but you give the impression that you are angry with him, and that is wrong. We are going to do this scene again, and Chris, please, before Ferapont enters and also in every pause, wonder, evaluate, make decisions and an expressive gesture. You see, we are trying to do what Chekhov did before he wrote the words for his characters. While a playwright studies all about the character—his thoughts, his images, his emotions, his whole inner world—he usually writes down only what the character says. We are trying to complete what the playwright left out. You should have an inner monologue while looking at Ferapont. What do you think while you are looking at him, Chris?

Chris: I have my inner monologue.

S.M.: Not every inner monologue may be right. You may have to change what you are wondering about quite often, not because I may suggest it, but because you yourself will be able to realize that something is wrong. Perhaps your objective must change or the behavior of your partner is different from what you expected. And, of course, your body must be expressive of what should be in your mind.

Some actors are unhappy when I say that they must do everything consciously on stage. They like to imagine themselves working subconsciously all the time. This is a great mistake, and one of the worst distortions of acting. The great Italian actor Salvini said: "An actor cries and laughs, and at the same time watches his crying and laughing." An actor who does not know what he is doing is not acceptable on stage. Otherwise there might be real murders on stage.

Conscious control does not hurt an actor's performance. On the contrary, it is obligatory. That is why I want you to learn control of your behavior from the very beginning; it should gradually become habitual. The scientist Pavlov said: "Isn't it quite natural that while we are busy with something, especially a thought, we can at the same time do something else that is a habit with us?" Constantly watch whether you are using the work you have prepared at home.

Do not listen to those who tell you that you must forget the audience. It is useless even to try. Stanislavski calls the audience the "co-creator" of a performance. You depend on its reactions. That does not mean that you must amuse the spectators. And you must also have them in mind when you analyze and study your role at home. You must carefully select the behavior that will be most expressive of the subtext of behavior, of what you want the audience to understand. You are working for the audience, for their understanding and pleasure.

S.M.: Control over your behavior is obligatory so that if errors do occur you will be able to correct them quickly. If your partner is really an actor of the Stanislavski school, he may be able to help you while continuing his own inner monologue and without stepping out of character. I hope you understand that our final objective is to achieve on stage a state of subconscious creativity, which is inspiration. *This* is our goal, rather than the conscious work. But conscious work is the means that prepares the most favorable ground for possible inspiration. Let us see the scene one more time.

> **Andrei**: Good evening, my good soul. What do you have to say?
>
> **Ferapont**: The chairman has sent you a book and some kind of paper. Here . . .
>
> **Andrei**: Thank you. Good. Why didn't you come earlier? It's already eight.
>
> **Ferapont**: Heh?
>
> **Andrei**: (*Louder*) I say, you came late. It's after eight already.

Ferapont: Yes sir. I came here, it was still light, but they wouldn't let me in. The master, they say, is busy. So what. Busy is busy. I have nowhere to hurry. Heh?

Andrei: Nothing. Tomorrow is Friday, I don't have to attend but I'll go anyway ... to occupy myself. It's boring at home ... (*Pause*) Dear Grandpa! How strangely life changes and deceives us! Today, out of boredom, because I had nothing else to do, I picked up this book—old university lectures—and I wanted to laugh ... My God, I'm a secretary of the District Board, the board where Protopopov is the chairman. I'm the secretary, and the most I can expect is to be a member of the District Board! I, the member of the District Board, I who dream every night that I am a professor at Moscow University, a famous scholar whom all of Russia is proud of!

Ferapont: I wouldn't know ... I don't hear well ...

Andrei: If you could I probably wouldn't talk to you. I need to talk to somebody, but my wife doesn't understand me, I'm afraid of my sisters for some reason. I'm afraid they'll laugh at me, embarrass me. I don't drink. I don't like saloons, but with what pleasure I would be sitting now at Testov's in Moscow, or in the Bolshoi Moscovsky, my dear fellow.

Ferapont: And in Moscow, the contractor at the District Board said some merchants were eating bliny; one who ate forty bliny, it seems, died. It was forty, or fifty. I don't remember.

Andrei: You sit in Moscow, in a huge salon at a restaurant, and no one knows you, and at the same time you don't feel like a stranger. And here you know everyone and you are known to everyone, but you are a stranger, a stranger and lonely.

Ferapont: Heh? (*Pause*) And the same contractor said— maybe he was lying—that a rope has been stretched across the whole of Moscow.

Andrei: What for?

Ferapont: I don't know. The contractor was saying.

Andrei: Rubbish. (*He reads.*) Have you ever been in Moscow?

Ferapont: (*After a pause*) Never been. God did not grant me that. (*Pause*) Shall I go?

Andrei: You may go. Keep well. (*Ferapont leaves.*) Keep well. (*Reading*) Tomorrow when you come, you will take some papers there . . . (*Pause*) He's left. (*Bell*) Yes, some business.

S.M.: Well, this is surprising progress. I saw a real effort to use your muscles and gestures. By the way, "bliny" means pancakes, and they are delicious!

Your leaning back in the chair with your arm on the back was very expressive. In order not to hear Ferapont's story about bliny, you must concentrate even more on wondering, evaluating, a decision, and a gesture. I would suggest that you continue to lean back, so that you are not so close to him. Chris, Andrei talks because he has no one to talk to. He is saying his inner monologue aloud. He does not cry yet. What are you as Andrei thinking when Ferapont talks about the rope being stretched across Moscow?

Chris: May I explain something about my inner monologue?

S.M.: Of course.

Chris: When Ferapont talks about the rope, I hear him

for the first time, and I am trying to understand and follow what he says. I am wondering and evaluating what I hear.

S.M.: Good. And yet, Ferapont's story about the rope would amuse Andrei. Well, give it a thought. Oh yes, your yawning at the end came as a surprise. I wouldn't do it. It is true that I have seen people yawn when they were nervous, but I have never seen Russians do this. (*Laughter*) The most important thing is that you were able to use the psychophysical work. Did you feel that the correct muscular movement in silences, or when you do not move, involved the right inner processes? I think that you were able to see a great many images. Is that true?

Chris: Yes, many of which I saw here today for the first time.

■ Class Five

SONIA MOORE: Good afternoon. Please turn your chairs so that you can see each other. You are on a bus. You do not know each other, but each of you observes the others without being noticed. Build the circumstances. Make sure also that you know why you are watching the other person. In life, if we observe someone, we know the reason—maybe the face seems familiar, and you are trying to remember where you could have met him, or you may recognize a thief, and so on. Follow the steps in your inner monologue and have an expressive gesture before and after you turn your head. Be aware of the obstacles to your objective and find ways to overcome them.

(The students perform the improvisation together.)

All right. That is enough. Now turn your backs to each other. Debbi, can you describe Kathy's clothes?

Debbi: She is wearing a brown pullover.

S.M.: Do you all agree that Kathy's pullover is brown? Is is brown, Kathy?

Kathy: No, it's green.

S.M.: Mat, please describe Jim's clothes.

Mat: He has on a white shirt and a black tie.

Jim: I have no tie at all.

S.M.: What color are his socks?

Mat: I don't know.

S.M.: Tom, can you help?

Tom: They are gray. I think he is wearing a ring and a pair of corduroy pants, sort of blue.

S.M.: Kathy, can you describe Sharon's clothes?

Kathy: Umm, no.

S.M.: I asked you to observe each other, though I did not tell you why, and you do not remember a thing. You must observe. You must observe yourself, and you must observe the world around you. And you must remember what you observe. You will use it again and again.

And now, everyone please come up to the table, all together. Put one hand on the table. Push up your sleeve, Chris. Put down the other hand, Kathy, the one without any rings or bracelets. Now examine all the hands closely. Then you will turn around, close your eyes, and try to guess by the touch whom they belong to. I shall count to twenty . . . All right. Everyone come upstage. Come here, Ruth. Stand at the table with your back to it. Come here (*pointing to another student*). Put your hand on the table. Ruth, you touch it, and tell us whose hand it is.

Touch it.

(*Ruth guesses right.*)

Good. You, Maria. Whose hand is this?

(*Maria guesses right.*)

But you should not walk so heavily because Maria recognized your footsteps. (*Laughter*) Don't help them to identify you.

Now you come to a friend to tell him some exciting news, and he is not at home. Do not rush on stage. You must know what the news is, who your friend is. Think why you want your friend to know about it. Remember an analogous emotion in your life. The situation does not have to be the same, but an analogous emotion is important. See in your mind all the people involved. They must be real people. Concentrate and build the situation.

(*Chris performs the improvisation.*)

S.M.: Chris, what you did physically was all wrong. You did many unnecessary things, and I did not believe that you saw people you know in life. I did not see you wondering, evaluating, or making a decision. What you did was not acting; it was indicating. The external means that you use to express what is inside must be economical; what is inside must be full.

Chris: I don't understand the difference between indicating and the use of gestures you describe. It seems to me in both cases I am using my body to express what I am feeling and thinking.

S.M.: No, because indicating is not acting; it is showing.

An actor who is indicating is showing the audience what his character is supposed to be feeling.

The gestures I am speaking about are part of a continuous psychophysical process. They are the result of an emotional state, and not simply a demonstration of it.

Let us see another improvisation.

(*Debbi performs the improvisation.*)

Why don't you leave after you find that your friend is not home?

Debbi: I could leave, but I want to wait and tell him the news.

S.M.: But he may not return for hours. Aren't there others whom you would like to tell? Wouldn't you try to reach your friend somewhere on the telephone or write a note?

Debbi: I just wanted to wait. I have a justification, but I guess it does not come through.

S.M.: No, it did not.

Let us work on *The Three Sisters*. Great effort is needed to change your psychological and physical behavior into the behavior of the character in a play. When you work on your character, you must also study your partner's lines. Most of the time you think in response to what you hear. This is how you learn the first steps of *ensemble* work. You wonder about what you hear, evaluate it, and make decisions.

In the scene at the beginning of the first act the three

sisters are separate. Each is immersed in her own world. But they love each other, and this should come through without hugging or kissing.

Let us do the scene with Joan as Irina, Kathy as Olga, and Ruth as Masha. We will start with the clock striking, which brings back memories of last year.

Listen to the sound, Kathy. It does not have to be the sound of a clock. Listen, really listen to a sound. Treat the sound you hear, even if it is a car outside, as if it were the clock. Take it in, i.e. wonder, evaluate, i.e. stir your feeling about it, make a decision, move strongly the muscles to which these mental processes are attached through paths of nerves in order to stir them, and project with a gesture what is in your mind; and then say the words. And in each pause continue the steps of your inner monologue. If the pause is brief condense it all into an expressive gesture. You must not have pauses that are unjustified and empty. This is a self-indulgent habit with some actors. As Stanislavski says, those pauses are for the actor's sake, not for the character's. Actors believe that such pauses are impressive, but they only create a void on stage because they kill the character's life. To be alive, there must be an uninterrupted flow of thought and emotion expressed through the body. This is what happens in life and creates spontaneity on stage. If you really stir your thoughts and emotions with the right muscles, you will not have dead pauses. Mental activity continues and expresses itself in pauses.

Joan, do not stand as if someone ordered you to stand there. Your physical expression does not correspond to what goes through your mind. You are supposed to be building dream castles, and you stand there like a schoolgirl being punished. Think of what pose would be right while standing there at the window or at the door to the terrace. Birds are singing and flowers are in bloom. . . . Good, yes, lean on the screen. Nobody has ordered you to stand there—you want to, and that must come across. Move upstage more. It would be difficult for us to believe that you do not hear Olga. Your concentration must be so strong that we believe you. It will be if you achieve psychophysical union.

Joan: I don't hear her even when she speaks of the funeral?

S.M.: You may come down to earth for a second and then go back to your dreams again. Masha is not listening either. Ruth, while working on Masha, you must study Olga's lines and decide when you hear her and what your thoughts are at those moments. Let us see the scene.

> **Olga (Kathy):** Father died exactly a year ago, on this very day, the fifth of May—your saint's day, Irina. It was cold, and snow was falling. It seemed to me that I would never live through it, and you were lying unconscious as if you were dead. And now a year later we can talk of it easily, you are already wearing a white dress, your face glows. (*A clock strikes twelve.*) And the clock was striking then, too. (*Pause*) It comes back to me that when father was carried away, music was playing and at the cemetery they fired a salute. He was a general, in command of a brigade, and yet there were only a few people. But it was raining then. Heavy rain, and snowing.
>
> **Irina (Joan):** Why remember?

Olga: Today it is warm. The windows can stay wide open, but the birches have no leaves yet. Father took command of the brigade and left Moscow with us eleven years ago, and I remember clearly that at the beginning of May in Moscow everything is already in bloom, everything is immersed in sunshine. Eleven years have passed, but I remember it all there as if we've left yesterday. My God, this morning I woke up and saw a flood of sunshine, saw the spring, and joy stirred in my soul, and I wanted passionately to go home.

Tchebutikin: (*Offstage*) Oh sure!

Tusenbach: (*Offstage*) Of course, nonsense.

(*Masha, pensive over her book, whistles softly.*)

Olga: Don't whistle, Masha—how can you! (*Pause*) It is because I'm at the high school every day and giving lessons till evening, that my head aches continually, and my thoughts are those of an old woman. Really, these four years I've been teaching, I have felt my strength and youth leaving me every day, drop by drop. And only one dream grows and strengthens. . . .

Irina: To leave for Moscow. Sell the house, to finish with everything here, and to Moscow.

Olga: Yes! To Moscow as soon as possible!

Irina: Brother will probably be a professor, and all the same he won't live here. Yet, the obstacle is poor Masha.

Olga: Masha will be coming to Moscow for the whole summer, every year.

(*Masha is softly whistling.*)

Irina: God willing, it all will work out. (*Looking out of the window*) The weather is good today. I don't know why my soul is so bright! This morning I remembered it was my saint's day and suddenly I felt joy, and I remembered my childhood when mother was still alive. And such marvelous thoughts stirred me, such thoughts.

Olga: Today you are radiant, you seem exceptionally beautiful. And Masha is beautiful, too. Andrei would be good looking, but he's gotten heavy, it's not becoming to him. And I've grown older and much thinner, probably because I get angry with the girls in school. I'm free today and am home and my head's not aching. I feel younger than yesterday. I'm only twenty-eight, only . . . it is all good, it all comes from God, but I feel that if I had married and stayed home all day, it would have been better. (*Pause*) I'd have loved my husband.

S.M.: Kathy, you are trying to see the images, but they are very pale; nobody else will see them. You must transmit them, your attitude to them, to your partners on stage through gestures. If you succeed in that, the audience will see them, too. When you work at home, go through your lines in your mind and see your partner in your mind. But never speak to an empty chair, because that will make you accustomed to receiving no reaction, and will eventually cause trouble when you do the scene with someone.

In life we have a certain attitude or feeling for everyone and everything. We have feelings about one another. We may largely be unaware of this, but I have a feeling about each of you, and you have one about me. When you transmit them to your partner in pauses through your gestures you create communion on stage. Kathy, when you have chosen the image for your father from among the people you know, you must have the same attitude about him that Olga has about her father. However, your father—Olga's father—died a year ago.

Today you are having a party for your sister Irina. It is not a funeral. Though Olga is not in the best of moods today, she is not mourning. Olga is strict with herself; she is dissolved in others; she has inner strength. She compares the situation today with the situation last year on the same day. Today marks the end of mourning and the determination to start a new life.

Kathy: But how can I speak without sadness when I am talking about such sad things?

S.M.: You are not sad. What you consider "sadness" is your own sympathy with Olga. Sadness is an emotion, and you cannot command it and be sad because the father of the character you are portraying is dead. Do not confuse your own sympathy, or the sympathy of an actress for the character, with the emotion of the character.

Kathy: Is it all right to see a person in mourning when I speak to Irina?

S.M.: If you did not look at Irina, it might be all right. But what you did is wrong. You must see Joan, who is our Irina. It is terrible to try to see someone else instead of the person who is in front of you. It is obligatory to *see* the actor who is performing with you, but to *treat* him as the character in the play. You do not have to look at her when you talk about her white dress, because she is your sister and you have seen her all morning. You can look at her afterward to admire her again, and then you see that her face is beaming. You may have images of people who do not appear *on* stage, but with a partner you must see *only* him or her. When you work at home, you can see a real person in your mind and find the typical actions that express your feelings. On stage, use those same actions to project your attitude toward your partner. I must emphasize this because I know how some of our actors do try to see people other than those with whom they are performing. Do you have any questions?

Tom: No, I don't, but I have a general awe of everything.

S.M.: Don't expect too much from yourselves. It is impossible to do everything perfectly all at once. We are in the process of learning how to stir our own emotions and transform them into those of the character, but you do not know how to do this yet. You must learn to fulfill psychophysical actions.

The first act of *The Three Sisters* starts with life vibrating, with high hopes, especially for Irina. Irina decides to go to work. She is like a little girl who has discovered that life is wonderful. Joan, you must find the right images and inner monologue for Irina, so that your face will be radiant without forced smiling. Why did you laugh?

Joan: Because yesterday I told Olga something funny, and remembering it made me laugh.

S.M.: I do not believe you. It looks to me as if you decided that this would be a good time to laugh.

Joan: Why shouldn't I laugh if I am happy?

S.M.: Happiness is also an emotion, and you cannot be happy only because you decide to be happy. But if you really remember something funny and find expressive gestures of your body, it would be perfectly all right. I do not expect you to do this correctly right now. What are your lines here?

Joan: "The weather is good today. I don't know why my soul is so bright."

S.M.: You see, you think that you must be happy, and you try to pretend to be. But instead of doing that, you must dig into your memory, find the right images, and know what should be on your mind. Movements of the right muscles will turn on these processes and make your eyes shine. It must be done at home and in classes. During a rehearsal you must use what you prepared at home, and we check whether what you have chosen is right. What you did just now looked empty. I am sure there are days when you wake up feeling especially good. Think of what you do then. We do not want just words, which rarely say what we think. You must be able to turn on your thoughts, and your body must express them.

And now, Masha. I would give a penny for your thoughts, Ruth. When Olga says, "Don't whistle, Masha," you looked totally blank. If you succeed in stirring the right thoughts, believe me, you can steal the show even though you are silent.

Ruth: I was blank, especially at the point you mentioned.

S.M.: Well, the problem is that inner monologue is impossible without muscles of the body turning it on. Please, work, make an effort to stir what should be in your mind with the muscles of your torso.

Let us see Baron Tusenbach's entrance.

> **Tusenbach (Tom)**: *(offstage)* You talk such nonsense, I became bored listening to you. *(Enters)* I forgot to say that our new battery commander, Vershinin, is going to call on you today.
>
> **Olga**: Well, I'll be very glad.
>
> **Irina**: Is he old?
>
> **Tusenbach**: No, at most forty or forty-five. Obviously a nice man. Not stupid, certainly. But he talks a great deal.
>
> **Irina**: Is he interesting?
>
> **Tusenbach**: Yes, not bad, but he has a wife, a mother-in-law, and two daughters. Moreover, he is married for the second time. He pays visits and tells everyone that he has a wife and two girls. And he'll say it here. The wife is somewhat crazy, with long girlish braids, and she uses pompous language, philosophizes, and often attempts to commit suicide, obviously to upset her husband. I'd have left her long ago, but he bears it and just complains.

S.M.: Tom, do not sit before Irina does. A Russian officer would not sit down before the ladies were all seated. Tusenbach is very much in love with Irina, and this should be clear when you enter the room. Tusenbach's speech is full of images. Did you work on images of Vershinin, his wife, and his two children, the mother-in-law? With this speech Veshinin is established for the first time. You must give a truly vivid description of the man. When you say, "not stupid, certainly," you must have specific words in mind that you heard Vershinin say which impressed you. You must express your feeling with a gesture before you say it.

Tom: I think I know what you want me to do.

S.M.: Good. Do you have an uncle?

Tom: Yes.

S.M.: How old is he?

Tom: About fifty.

S.M.: How tall is he?

Tom: Oh, about five feet eleven.

S.M.: Do you think you see Vershinin and his family in your mind the way you see your uncle now? Wonder, evaluate, decide, and make an expressive gesture before and after you say, "No, at most forty or forty-five," about Vershinin.

Tom: Yes, I understand, but it's not easy.

S.M.: No, it is not. Your gestures must be more expressive. I do not see Vershinin's wife when you describe her, neither do I see his mother-in-law. Do not rush. It looks as if you want to be through with it, instead of working and making your images clear to these three women.

Ruth: Mrs. Moore, I have a question about inner monologue. When he describes the person, am I supposed to have other thoughts in my wondering, evaluating and deciding that may not be related to the person he describes?

S.M.: If you think that would be logical for the moment on stage, it is all right. If you are listening to him, then you should have thoughts, images, and feelings related to what he says and what you hear. However, when you are trying to concentrate on the book, you may be thinking of what is disturbing you.

Talk to all the sisters, Tom. Make sure your partners understand you and believe you. Tusenbach is an intelligent man, and he has a sense of humor. And Olga, Masha, and Irina, I do not want to see any mechanical movements of your heads looking at each other or at Tusenbach. This is what most actors do. While Tusenbach is speaking you must have your own images of what he describes.

Ruth: Don't you think that Masha is interested only for a moment in what Tusenbach says, and then she goes back to her book?

S.M.: Yes, you are right. And Olga, too, listens only for a while and then continues correcting her papers. I do not insist that you should think all the time in reaction to what Tusenbach is saying, but in pauses you must think as Olga without interruption. And the same thing applies to Masha. You don't have to listen to him all the time, but that does not mean that there can be dead moments.

You must wonder, evaluate, and make decisions continually.

Irina is the one who is listening attentively to the baron. Now your face becomes really radiant, Joan. But still you must change your inner monologue somewhat. When you are wondering, evaluating, and making decisions, the audience must see at the start that you are daydreaming. Your face becomes radiant only during Olga's speech. Why don't you use the same thoughts at the very beginning? And you do not have to *tell* your sisters that your brother "will probably be a professor." They know this. You are dreaming aloud. Try the scene again.

(The scene is performed again.)

Joan, you must change your images. You are still looking uncomfortable and unhappy.

Kathy, you're not mourning any more, but now you are overdoing it in another direction, and I don't believe you.

Kathy: I decided that although it had been cold and snowing, now it is warm, and this excites me.

S.M.: You cannot be excited just because you have decided to be. You are overdoing it. Remember what we call the measure of truth. Also, when you looked out the window, you did not wonder, evaluate, or make any decision. You looked and looked before you said that the birches haven't any leaves yet, as if you had to make sure. But Olga knows this. She goes outside every day. It looked terribly overdone. For Olga everything in Moscow is wonderful, and everything here is bad. You even pretended to be surprised when you looked out the window. Still, most of it was much better.

Kathy: My images are becoming clearer.

S.M.: Yes, especially in the beginning and the middle of the speech—I'm sure of it. It is because you moved the right muscles. This time you really worked. You have made definite progress. Continue your work on transmitting your images to your partners.

Irina, what passes through your mind after you say, "Why remember?" Irina does not stop daydreaming even then. Be sure that you use expressive gestures before you say it and after you have said it, but only to express what words cannot express, the inner experiences.

■ Class Six

SONIA MOORE: Let us perform something new. Joan, come here behind everyone. All of you sit as you are, don't turn around. You will have to guess by the sound what Joan is doing. All right, let us begin.

Kathy: She is erasing something.

S.M.: No, do it again, Joan. What is she doing? Your effort to understand the sound is important.

Mat: She is dusting the table. With a cloth.

S.M.: That is right. Come here, Tom, and take Joan's place. I want you all to guess what he is doing.

Ruth: Isn't he taking a Kleenex out of a box?

S.M.: Yes, very good. Do you realize that you were all wondering, evaluating, making decisions and expressive gestures?
And now a sense-memory exercise. You will "thread a needle." You must "see" what you are doing; concentrate on it; feel the objects you imagine; know their weight. This is an especially useful exercise because it teaches you to be concrete in your actions. Your actions must be so truthful that the audience really believes that

you are threading a needle. I want you all to criticize each other. Since you know that every action will be different in different circumstances, I want you to build the circumstances in these exercises, too. For instance, if you are a tailor and sew all day long, your action of threading the needle will be different than if you are dressing for a party and a button falls off your shirt. The important thing is to fulfill a single purposeful action in the given circumstances, and you better learn to do it from the beginning.

(*The exercise is performed.*)

You know when I thread a needle, first I have to take out the box, find the needle and thread. But when you do it, everything seems to be right at your hand.

Now an improvisation. You are "preparing to go to a reception." It is important for you to be there on time. In building the situation see real people you know in life whom you expect to meet there. When you are ready to leave, you find a note under the door. That is all I am going to tell you now. I will put a real note there. Before picking it up, wonder, evaluate, make a decision and a summarizing gesture. Then you move and pick it up, and make another expressive gesture. Read it, execute the psychophysical steps, and make a meaningful gesture. Remember an analogous emotion in life. Stir mental activity with the muscles of your torso.

Tom: There will be something written on it?

S.M.: Yes, and you must make a decision after you have read it. It is important for you to be at the reception, and you must know why it is important.

Tom: You want us to mime the work?

S.M.: What do you mean by "mime"?

Tom: I mean, do you want us to do this without props?

S.M.: No, this is an improvisation. I have asked you to always use props except in the sense-memory exercises. Sense-memory exercises teach you to be so thoroughly concrete that we will be able to see objects that don't exist. But if you do not use real objects in the other exercises and improvisations, your actions will be vague, and you will undermine the concreteness we are trying to create.

Don't think how you are going to do the improvisation before you have built the circumstances. The way you dress would depend on where you were going and whom you were expecting to meet; perhaps it is an influential agent, or maybe a producer. Go on stage as soon as you are ready. When you read the note, do what you would do if this were happening in life. And do not tell us afterward what you were doing! We must understand from your actions. Remember the psychophysical steps and the meaningful gestures. Do not tell anyone else what the note says.*

(*Improvisation by Jim*)

That was good, Jim. The note obviously disturbed you. Your muscles stirred the inner processes, and your rushing out with your tie still undone was very expressive. You know, little by little you begin behaving on stage like

---

*The note reads: "Your best friend has been in a serious auto accident and is at Roosevelt Hospital. Hurry."

normal human beings. Almost everyone has some extra skins that must be shed. You are beginning to look like your own selves. The System helps you to reach the core of your own personality. Only when you reach yourself will you be able to build other people. Did you see real people in your mind? Good. Who is next? Put the note back where it was there on the floor. Thank you.

(*Improvisation by Sharon*)

Sharon, you did not seem interested in what you read in the note. And why did you take your book along with you?

Sharon: Well, I take this book everywhere with me.

S.M.: Carrying the book does not help to project that you are going to a reception. Only behavior that helps to express the situation is artistic; the rest only confuses the audience. They say Stanislavski once asked Rachmaninoff what accounted for the mastery of a pianist, and Rachmaninoff answered, "Not touching the neighboring key." And the actor's mastery is in not using anything beyond what is strictly necessary.

(*Improvisation by Joan*)

Joan, you, too, just walked out without giving a thought, no wondering, no evaluation of what you read in the note. Your tempo-rhythm did not change at all. In life the slightest change of circumstances changes the objectives, and it stirs a different tempo-rhythm. After reading such news in life you would stop and decide what to do. I would like to see it again, please.

(*Joan repeats the improvisation.*)

Now that was better.

Let us work on *The Three Sisters* now. We shall move on to the scene between Tusenbach and Soliony with John as Tusenbach and Dan as Soliony. Are you seeing the images while you speak? Are you concentrating on the steps of your inner monologue when you are not speaking? Is the inner monologue stirred by the muscles around your spine? Do you know why you are saying your lines? And are you projecting with your body what the words cannot project—that is, the subtext? And remember there must be no empty pauses interrupting your wondering, evaluating, deciding, gesturing, and the physical action that follows.

Try the scene.

Tusenbach (John): You always sit by yourself, thinking about something—

S.M.: (*Interrupting*) Dan, did you hear Tusenbach's footsteps?

Dan: No.

S.M.: You must have heard them. I did.

Dan: I was thinking.

S.M.: I was thinking, too. We are always thinking in life, but we still see and hear what happens around us.

Dan: I heard some movement.

S.M.: There must be a physical reaction, a gesture.

Otherwise you seem deaf and dead. Soliony has become annoyed with Natasha and with himself and has left the dining room and wants to be alone. But as soon as he sits down, someone comes in after him. You did not hear Tusenbach coming because you did not achieve psychophysical involvement in this situation; you were paralyzed. Try the scene again.

> **Tusenbach:** You always sit by yourself, thinking about something—no one could tell what it was. Well, let's make peace. Let's drink some cognac. I'll probably have to play the piano all night long, play all kinds of nonsense. Come what may!
>
> **Soliony:** Why make peace? We haven't quarreled.
>
> **Tusenbach:** You always make me feel that something has gone wrong between us. You have a strange disposition, I must say.
>
> **Soliony:** (*declamatory*) I am strange, and who is not strange? Don't be angry, Aleko!
>
> **Tusenbach:** And what has Aleko to do . . . (*Pause*)
>
> **Soliony:** When I'm alone with someone, it's all right, I'm like everyone else, but in company I'm despondent, shy, and . . . talk all sorts of nonsense. And yet I am more honest and noble than many, many others. I can prove it.
>
> **Tusenbach:** I'm often angry with you, you never stop nagging at me when we're in company, and still for some reason I like you. Come what may, I shall get drunk today. Let's drink!
>
> **Soliony:** Let's drink. I've never had anything against you, Baron. But I have the disposition of Lermontov. I even resemble Lermontov somewhat, they say. (*Takes a bottle of perfume from his pocket and pours some over his hands.*)
>
> **Tusenbach:** I'm going to resign. Basta! For five years I

couldn't make up my mind, and now I've decided. I shall go to work.

Soliony: (*declamatory*) Don't be angry, Aleko. Forget, forget your dreams.

Tusenbach: I shall go to work.

S.M.: Your objective is not clear, John. You look as if you were telling Soliony, "Well, go ahead with your lines, so I can say mine."

John: I am thinking he is a strange fellow. Should I change it?

S.M.: Project it with a gesture. It does not come through, your muscles do not move. Your inner monologue must be stirred through the muscles of your torso.

John: But how can I have an inner monologue and talk at the same time?

S.M.: You must not have an inner monologue while you are speaking. When you speak you must project the meaning and see the images. The inner monologue is used during pauses in your own lines or when other people speak on stage. It is in silences that you must wonder, evaluate, make decisions and gestures. And you must move the muscles in silences. When you speak you must restrain your body. Also, John, when you say "Let's drink," and clink glasses, why don't you drink then?

John: I am not sure what kind of a man Tusenbach is. I

was ready to scream at him.

S.M.: You might scream, but Tusenbach would not. Tusenbach is always in good spirits, and he radiates goodness. Yes, in order to give Soliony justification for saying, "Don't be angry, Aleko," you must react in a psychophysical way to what he has said. But Tusenbach is not angry; Soliony just annoys him.

Dan, do not look at Tusenbach when you start the confession all of a sudden.

Dan: I am supposed to talk to him.

S.M.: Yes, you should be talking to him, but you do not have to look at him. We don't always look at a person when we speak to him. And before you say, "When I am alone, I am all right," you must wonder, evaluate, and make a decision and a gesture before and after you speak. Soliony softens and talks about his troubles to another man. Then, when you see that Tusenbach agrees with your self-criticism, you fall back into your usual self and tell him that you are not any worse than he.

Learn to react continuously to each other in a psychophysical way. Study your partner's lines and know your reactions. Though you look at him, Dan, believe me, you are not talking to Tusenbach. There is no way for us to know what you are saying or doing, and why. You isolate yourself; you lose contact with your partner and everything around you. You must learn to stir your own emotions to function in the character's circumstances.

If you do not project the action, first, you will never involve your psychophysical apparatus; second, the audience will not identify your character; and thus third, the audience has no idea of what is happening on stage. Thus your presence on stage makes no sense at all.

Dan: Why can't I stir the emotions of the character?

S.M.: Because a character in a play is dead until an actor's own emotions, will, memory, thoughts, and body are involved. This is your material for creating another person.

Dan: I don't think we have to try to bring out an actor's emotions, because an actor already has his own emotions.

S.M.: Yes, when it concerns his own personal interests. When the interests are those of the character in a play, an actor's emotions will not come to the surface spontaneously. The Stanislavski System will give you the possibility of stirring your own emotions for the character.

Dan: I've studied acting in New York for five years . . .

S.M.: Stanislavski studied for forty years! He never hesitated to demolish the means that he himself had established when he found better ones. If you don't change your attitude as quickly as possible you will remain an amateur for the rest of your life. That is a pity. One more thing. You also resent that we dwell on the same scene for such a long time.

Dan: I do—because it becomes stale.

S.M.: I thought so. With the Stanislavski technique, a role can never become sta_e. It is when you mechanically say your lines, repeat just any form, that it is dead. But Stanislavski says, "Today, now, here." If you do all the work anew every time, it will be always fresh, and your role will grow. You will find more and more interesting things. Stanislavski gives an actor unlimited possibilities.

■ Class Seven

SONIA MOORE: Listen carefully to the numbers I give: Your neck is number one; shoulder, number two; arms, three; torso, four; hands, five; legs, six; feet, seven. *Relax* number seven; relax number one; relax number three; relax number six; relax number four. This exercise also helps to develop your concentration.

John and Joan, come on stage. You are at the opera together. Think of real tunes. Try to see images of a specific opera. Dan, come here. You are at the same opera, but you are alone. You happen to see Joan's face and are trying to remember where you have seen her. You wonder, evaluate, make decisions and gestures. Find the right muscles. You must see real places, real people you know in life, at parties you have attended.

Dan: While the opera is going on?

S.M.: Right. While you are trying to remember where you could possibly have met her, you are unable to concentrate on the performance. John and Joan, you are disturbed by Dan's attention. You two, decide on the situation: Who are you two to each other? You may be engaged, you may be husband and wife. Your attitude to Dan will depend on your relationship. React to the person who disturbs you in the opera as you would in life, in a psychophysical way. Wonder, evaluate, and make decisions that will be stirred through your muscles. And select meaningful gestures.

> (*Improvisation. Joan and John take seats side by side, glance at their programs, "listen." Dan sits near Joan, looks at her, evidently in hope that she will look at him. He drops his program to gain attention. John and Joan, pretending not to notice him, change places.*)

John: I couldn't keep a straight face during what Dan was trying to do. I just felt like, oh, he's giving Joan a dirty look. When I looked at Joan, I started to laugh, too, and as a result I did not work enough.

S.M.: Your body and your mind are not ready, and this is understandable. It will become easier and easier as you gain control over your muscles. You have already learned something. Every day we see some improvement.

Another improvisation. You are "looking over an apartment that you want to rent." You may need an apartment for different reasons. You probably have looked for an apartment; if you have not, use the "magic IF." Do not think about how to do it until you know why you want the apartment. Are you getting married, or have you quarreled with your parents or your roommate? The event must be important. The situation will dictate your actions. Is everyone ready? Mat, go on.

(*Improvisation*)

S.M.: (*whispering to Dan*) Are you ready? Then go into the same apartment while Mat is in there looking it over.

(*Mat and Dan look over the apartment.*)

Mat, you should know better than to make faces. If you had really thought and your gestures had expressed it, we would understand whether you liked the apartment or not without your making faces.

I cannot succeed in keeping two people on stage. As soon as someone else comes on, the first person disappears! You know, Dan came on stage and walked around for a while, and you behaved as if he did not exist. It was as if Dan were a ghost. If you were really looking over an apartment and someone else came in who wanted it, you would behave in a different way. If I had liked an apartment, I would have tried to guess what the other person thought of it. But you didn't even see him.

You must learn to be aware of other people. Stay for a while, then make up your mind about the apartment and leave.

And now you will prepare a room in the house where you work as a housekeeper. Your employers are expecting guests. You may not have worked as a housekeeper, but you may have had to do something for someone you disliked. Think of the physical state. Think of an analogous emotion. The situation does not have to be the same. Are you ready, Pat?

(*Pat performs the improvisation.*)

That was good, Pat. But did you see real people whom you work for? Maybe these people's children are always leaving the room dirty, and you constantly have to clean up after them. When the Moscow Art Theatre was here, their director came to see our work, and later he said to me, "Sonia, please, continue to concentrate on simple actions in concrete circumstances." And he also said, "I know that you are doing the right thing because your students' eyes are alive."

If you fulfill an action without using the circumstances, it has no meaning. If your physical actions have been selected thoroughly to disclose the circumstances you have built, if you used the muscles necessary to stir mental processes, you would not have failed to see images. In this improvisation, if you like the people you work for, your cleaning will be different than if you hate them. It will be different if these people have parties all the time and you are tired. You will do it in a different way if you have decided to quit working for them. *How* you do it will make the audience understand what is taking place on stage.

(*Kathy performs the improvisation.*)

S.M.: (*To the other students*): What did you understand?

Debbi: When she looked at those shoes, I thought they were some other woman's, and when she looked at the bottle, I thought she wanted to finish it, but it was not clear.

S.M.: That's right. There was a hint of that, but not enough gestures of the body to project it clearly. Kathy, did you like the family you worked for?

Kathy: I was hired to clean a bachelor's apartment, and it was a mess, and I saw that pair of shoes.

S.M.: In life, seeing those shoes, you would gesture spontaneously, but on stage you must consciously use your muscles.

Kathy: I was afraid you'd think I was indicating.

S.M.: If you fulfill the psychophysical action, it is never an indication, because you function organically. These improvisations force you to think logically and thus develop your imagination. Without a fertile imagination, your work on stage is impossible.

Now you are "packing." Know your objective, build the circumstances. Why are you packing? Where are you going? Are you going alone? Are you packing at home? In a hotel? Build all the details you can imagine and then find characteristic actions of packing to reveal the situation to us. In a play your role is not ready until you know what you are doing and why you are doing it at every moment on stage.

(*Sharon performs the improvisation.*)

I would like to understand what you were doing. What was there near the window?

Sharon: A painting. I had to leave right away, and I wanted to say something to my friend, and she was not there.

S.M.: What does all this have to do with packing?

Sharon: I was leaving this place, and I wanted to bring in the circumstances.

S.M.: Why did you lie down on the floor?

Sharon: I just associated lying on the carpet and looking at the painting with this whole place.

S.M.: What you did only cluttered the situation and confused us. I think I understand from what you are saying that you did not want to part with the painting.

Sharon: I didn't take enough time to bring it all out. I was thinking of music and of some of my friend's things, and they didn't coordinate. I failed because I was not concentrating on specific actions.

S.M.: Absolutely correct. Thank you.
   Something new. Come into the room, stand on the chair, go down on your knees, and run out.

Mat: We enter the room. Why?

S.M.: Build your circumstances, justify every moment, and make sense of it.

Robert: We go down on our knees on the chair or the floor?

S.M.: On the floor. Are you ready? Go on.
   (*Maria performs the improvisation.*)
   What were you doing? First, you seemed to be looking in the mirror.

Maria: I was looking in the mirror.

S.M.: But then you seemed to be praying.

Robert: Yes, she was—weren't you? Were you going to a wedding?

Maria: Well, I was going somewhere that was important to me and that could change my whole life. I wanted to make sure that everything would be all right, so I prayed.

S.M.: We understood that you were looking in the mirror and that you were praying, but we didn't understand why. Be more specific. Find the right muscles and meaningful gestures.
(*Pat performs the improvisation.*)
What was it?

Pat: A mouse.

S.M.: I don't believe that you would do in life what you did just now. You would probably run away or get something to hit it with. You don't go down on your knees when you see a mouse.
And now a sense-memory exercise, which, of course, is done without objects. We will "carry a full pail of water" across the room. You must see the pail in your mind, feel its weight, handle it so truthfully that we will see it, too.
(*Chris carries an imaginary pail of water.*)

S.M.: (*to other students*) Are you satisfied? (*No answer*) Well, I am not. I do not think it was full at all.

Chris: It was half full.

S.M.: Then do it again with a full pail. (*Laughter. Chris performs the improvisation again.*)

That is much better. Were you carrying water to help put out a fire? Or was it for the operating room of a hospital?

Chris: How do I project that I am carrying this pail across the room to wash the floor, say?

S.M.: Couldn't you, for instance, sweep the floor first or pour water on it—after taking in the situation, evaluating, and making a decision? Stirring mental activity with your muscles and important gestures of the body would help us to understand what you want to do. You were just standing there with the pail.

Chris: I see now.

S.M.: Every improvisation should help you learn to fulfill a simple action in concrete circumstances. A psychophysical action will involve your inner experience and make the situation in the play clear to the audience at every moment.

You build a character with actions. For example, you know that there is a child in a house on fire, and you are bringing the pail of water to help extinguish the fire to save the baby. If, for instance, you see the fire and don't care, your actions will project a certain kind of person. On the other hand, if you see the fire and rush to help, you project another kind. If you throw things around, you project one character; if you are neat, you project another. Such actions, also called *adaptations*, are for actors what paint is for painters, Stanislavski said.

I think I have made it clear why even in a sense-memory exercise I want you to build the circumstances.

Let us try another sense-memory exercise: "to hang a picture." Again you must build the circumstances—what kind of a picture it is: a Renoir, a Raphael, or a cheap reproduction. Do not stop wondering, evaluating, making decisions, stirring the inner monologue with your muscles. Make an expressive, summarizing gesture before you make the movement to hang the picture, and after you have hung it.

(*Jim performs the exercise.*)

Was that the Mona Lisa or another famous painting that you stole from the Louvre?

Jim: Yes, yes.

S.M.: You used a great deal of imagination. Everything you did was crystal clear. However, don't you think that your picture changed size every now and then? All right, who's next?

(*Robert performs the exercise.*)

What do you think of that? Don't be afraid to criticize. You will be criticized; it makes you observe and learn.

Ruth: What was he pounding into the wall? It did not look like a nail.

Robert: No, it was a thumbtack. (*Laughter*)

S.M.: Can you hang a picture on a thumbtack? You see how we forget the simplest things on stage?

Robert: Couldn't it have been a long tack with a head that you had to screw in?

S.M.: This is a very important exercise because it helps you learn to fulfill an action thoroughly and concretely. This is what you must do in a role. Everything must be specific and expressive.

Debbi: Let me tell you what has been happening to me since I have been doing these exercises. I notice the gestures I make while I am working. Even if I only pick up a book from a table I find myself analyzing. If I have to cross a room I feel as if I'm performing. I constantly wonder and evaluate. I am very much aware of everything.

S.M.: Very good.

Debbi: Before I would just walk across the room. Now I wonder. (*Laughter*)

S.M.: You will see how that will help you when you start to work on roles. Observing and studying yourself and others is most important for your work.

Now, an improvisation: you are "coming home after a day in the mine." Yes, you have spent a whole day underground. Know your objective; build the circumstances. There may be different reasons why you were in the mine. Are you in your home town, on a trip? Are you living alone? And so on.

While working on an improvisation, never try to "act." Think of an analogous emotion. Think of what

you did or would do if you had been in a mine for eight hours. If you want your action to be truthful, you must achieve psychophysical involvement.
(*John performs the improvisation.*)

S.M.: John, why were you looking at me every now and then? Obviously you were not concentrating on what you were doing.

John: I have never been in a mine.

S.M.: But I am sure you have done heavy or dirty work sometime. Well, who is next?
(*Several students perform the improvisation.*)
What do you think of Kathy's improvisation?

Tom: I thought she looked sad instead of tired. When somebody's tired, he isn't sad; he has kind of a blank look.

S.M.: Kathy, you were pretending to be sad. You must not try to be sad, but remember an analogous emotion when you were sad and move the right muscles. This will stir the emotion of sadness in you now.
(*More students perform the improvisation.*)

S.M.: What do you think was wrong?

Jim: I did not see any difference between Ruth walking toward the sink to wash and walking away afterward.

S.M.: You walked into the house in dirty overalls and then took them off and put them in a drawer. Yes, that was funny. It was clear to us that those were the overalls you worked in. Maybe you were too tired to take them off before coming home. But you do not go to the table in dirty clothes, and you do not put them in a drawer. Don't you think you might have taken them off outside? Your choice was not believable. You would never have behaved this way in life. In addition you touched the chair several times with filthy hands, and only after that did you go to wash them. Who is next?

(*Improvisation by Jim*)

You seemed to be wiping your hands on your shirt. You looked quite brisk, and then all of a sudden, you seemed tired and went outside for some reason. There was no taking in, no evaluating or making decisions.

Jim: I went outside to brush off my clothes.

S.M.: Don't you think you should have done that before you came in?

(*Improvisation by Joan*)

Mat: She looked as if she had just seen an accident in the street.

John: We couldn't tell at all that she was in a mine.

Joan: I saw a man killed in a mine.

S.M.: Was he a man you really know in life? You know that you must use images of people you really know in all the improvisations.

Now we shall "burn a letter." What kind of letter is it? Who sent it to you? Why are you burning it? Remember the steps in your inner monologue and the expressive gestures. See real people in your mind.
(*Improvisation by Sharon*)
What were you burning?

Sharon: A letter from a close friend.

S.M.: Why were you reading that book before you burned the letter?

Sharon: Well, I was trying to study for an examination.

S.M.: Sharon, tell me what reading the book has to do with burning the letter.

Sharon: Nothing, I guess.

S.M.: If you projected that you were trying to concentrate on the book in order not to think of the letter, that would have been fine, because you would have been overcoming an obstacle.

Chris: Now I understand what you mean by saying we must not have too many objectives.

S.M.: I beg your pardon? Did I say that? (*Laughter*) In a play we have the superobjective of the author, and all the actions—*the through line of actions*—must contribute gradually to disclosing it. Every action must have an objective or it stops being human behavior. How do spectators understand a play? Through consecutive, logical, and expressive actions.

If an action is not helpful, eliminate it. Keep only what has to be projected. If you want to read a book because you have to study for an exam, it is perfectly all right, but we must understand that you are unable to concentrate on the book *because* you are disturbed by the letter.

Chris: I thought at first that she was going to find the letter in the book.

Debbi: You know, I thought that she was trying to be very cool and calmly sit there and read the book while the letter was burning. I thought she was trying to prove something to herself.

S.M.: Everyone here had a different idea of what you were doing.

John: The main action was reading the book—not burning the letter.

S.M.: Right. That is what came through. Can you imagine how important it is on stage to know how to choose the right actions? Anybody else ready?
(*Improvisation by Joan*)
Joan? Are you a spy?

Joan: The letter was from a woman for whom I worked.

S.M.: It is very important that you yourself know all the circumstances, and they must be expressed. The people in the audience must not have to strain to understand what is taking place. You will burn the letter differently if it is from a lover than if it is an important document that is dangerous for you to keep. The richer your imagination, the richer your adaptations will be, and the more interesting your work will be. For the moment, I am happy if you are able to project in the simplest way what is taking place in the circumstances you have built. But, as I have already told you, in the theatre not every truth is interesting. You know, the great actor Michael Chekhov wanted to be a writer before he became an actor. He wrote a story and showed it to his mother, who read it and said, "It is very truthful, but it is not interesting." (*Laughter*) The more your imagination develops, the more demanding I shall become.

(*Improvisation by Ruth*)
Why were you looking at the door?

Ruth: I know that I was not getting it across. My lover was waiting for me, and this was a note from him. My husband and children were in the other room.

S.M.: Your looking at the door was not convincing. I am sure that if this paper were something you weren't supposed to have, you would either have closed the door or at least made sure that no one was near. Would you really have burned this if your husband and children were in the next room?

Ruth: I knew all the circumstances, but there was no way

I could show them to you without indicating.

S.M.: Purposeful actions will never be indications if they are dictated by the circumstances.
  (*Improvisation by Dan*)
  And what did you burn?

Dan: I didn't know whether I was going to burn this letter or not.

S.M.: Where was your inner conflict? How was it expressed?

Dan: I'm alone in my room. There's no one for me to express it to.

S.M.: On the contrary, precisely *because* you are alone in your room without anyone watching, you might do a great deal that would have expressed your inner experience. I want you to make an effort to think about either what you did in such a case in life, or what you would do if it should happen. In life the whole complex inner world of a human being is always being expressed physically. On stage you must learn to find the muscles attached to the inner experiences in order to stir and convey the turmoil inside you. When you find such a muscle and move it, it triggers the emotion you need and you achieve psychophysical involvement. When you succeed, your whole organic nature will be involved: your senses, your memory, your will, your emotions, your thoughts, your body. Then you behave on stage as a living human being.

Dan: Well, what if in life you don't show expression. I know people like that.

S.M.: Take it for a rule, Dan—there always is some physical expression, even if it is only a movement of a muscle.

Dan: In life, you could watch every movement someone made, and you wouldn't have the faintest idea what he was doing. On stage, there would have to be more to it.

S.M.: Start watching yourself in life, Dan; it is difficult to convince you with words alone. I am certain that if you were alone while burning the letter, you would be doing much more than just sitting there with a blank expression in your eyes. You would be wondering, evaluating, making decisions and gestures.

Dan: In my circumstances I cannot show it to you.

S.M.: What do you mean, "show"?

Dan: Just because it's theatre, do I have to walk around and make a lot of unnecessary movements to show you exactly what I'm doing when the whole point is that I'm not interested in showing anybody? (*Laughter*) I am just sitting here and reading the letter, and I'm trying to decide whether I'm going to burn it or not, and I finally decide to burn it, and that's exactly—

S.M.: But nothing came through, Dan. Your muscles did not move, and that's why you did not stir these processes or project them. You seem to be one of those actors who think that people should be content to see Dan sitting there for no reason at all, and they should all applaud just for the pleasure of seeing you. Watch yourself in life, and watch those around you. Once you have made your observations and then verified them, come back and report to us. We will all be very interested.

Stanislavski verified everything many times, experimenting with himself and his actors, and sought confirmation from scientists. The only reason for your being on stage is to make everything crystal clear to your audience, and if you do not, you will not satisfy them or your director.

Dan: The audience knows the circumstances, they know what has gone before. Anyhow, it is absolutely impossible to make clear to the audience all the details of a situation.

S.M.: Then make clear as many details as you are capable of expressing now, today. Tomorrow, you may have another detail to add. Next week, another. But accept the process, Dan. It will open a new world to you and your audience. May we try one step at a time?

Dan: OK.

S.M. Thank you.

■ Class Eight

SONIA MOORE: Dan, please go into the front room and close the door after you. (*Whispering*) Let us make some changes here. Kathy, take off your jacket and put it on the chair. (*Mrs. Moore suggests several other changes.*) Dan, come back now. Look around carefully and tell us whether you notice any changes. This is not just a game. It is a way to develop your ability to observe. There is unlimited material for observation around us in life.

Dan: Sharon put her coat on. Didn't she put her coat on?

S.M.: No.

Dan: John was holding a book.

S.M.: He still is, Dan.

Dan: Mat is sitting on a pillow.

S.M.: He was sitting on that pillow all the time. Do you give up? But first try again to remember. Don't you see that Kathy and Joan exchanged chairs?

Joan: And we put an ashtray on your chair.

S.M.: All right. Now you go, Ruth. Maria, put this jacket on. No, don't put Ruth's coat on. She would have to be blind not to notice. Come back, Ruth.
(Ruth does not notice any changes.)

S.M.: Do you give up?

Ruth: Yes.

S.M.: Don't you see that John, sitting there next to you, has rolled his sleeves up? Both of them? (*Laughter*)

Ruth: Oh yes, and Maria put on this jacket.

S.M.: Right, and one more thing. Everyone is participating, so look at everybody. You see, I am trying to help you.

Ruth: Oh, there is a suitcase on this table. And you took off your bracelet.

S.M.: Good. Now we shall perform an improvisation with music. We'll play a record—Beethoven's First Symphony. You are all on the beach of a fisherman's village. There has been a terrible storm during the night. Dawn is breaking now, and you are waiting for—your husband, brother, father, son, friend? Think also of your relationship to those who are on the beach with you. Listen to the music and use it as one of the circumstances. This is an improvisation for everyone together. Watch your blocking. Do not block others, and see that you are not blocked.

It is early morning; you have been waiting on the beach for hours. . . .

(*Improvisation*)

All right, thank you. You could have used the music in a more effective way. I purposely played it soft and then loud, but only Robert paid attention—he ran forward and started waving, as if he heard voices. Kathy, you were so busy being "sad" that when you sat next to Joan you didn't notice she was crying. You did not pay attention even when she asked you for a tissue. This proves that you did not achieve a psychophysical state, and that is why you did not react to the world around you as you would in life.

Now, one of you go on stage. Enter a room ready to "meet an unknown person." As always, build the circumstances. Concentrate. All right, Robert, I see that you are ready.

(*Robert enters and pantomimes speech.*)

Please do not talk to anyone who is not there.

Robert: How do I know that he is not there?

S.M.: Can't you see that he is not there? (*Laughter*) Try to behave as you do in life. If no one is there, you have no one to talk to.

(*Debbi performs the improvisation.*)

Who did you come to meet? It was not very clear.

Debbi: A friend.

S.M.: Didn't I say to "meet an unknown person?"

The next improvisation will be "two people who are

not on speaking terms." Talk over the situation between you. First decide with whom you will do it. Know your relationship—why you are not on speaking terms. Know what emotion you must reach. Do not speak or pantomime. There should be no need to talk. As soon as there is an organic need to speak, the improvisation is finished. After you have built the situation, go on, and do not "make an entrance." Come on stage for a purpose. Life goes on off stage and must continue on stage.

(*John and Tom perform the improvisation.*)

Well, I am sure you would not be glancing at each other all the time as you did. What was it, anyway? Did you want to make up after a quarrel? Were you friends living in the same room?

John: He had dated my best girlfriend, and I did not know it, and then I found out. I couldn't find anything to do and concentrated on my feelings.

S.M.: You should also concentrate on muscles—that would stir the feelings Finding the right muscles will stir the right emotions.

John: Without saying anything?

S.M.: I know it's very difficult.

John: I found it difficult to concentrate because of my tremendous anger and hurt.

S.M.: Oh, you think that you were angry and hurt? An actor can be hurt or angry without a personal reason if he has learned the technique of involving his whole psychophysical apparatus. You certainly have no personal reason to be hurt, because Tom did not take your girlfriend away from you. What you think were your emotions was only physical tension.

(*Chris and Debbi perform the improvisation.*)

My, how stingy you are!

Chris: Mrs. Moore understood it! Was it clear that I hated writing all those checks?

S.M.: Yes, the way you looked over at her as you wrote them and the evaluating made it clear. But Debbi, are you really a spendthrift, or is he just stingy?

Debbi: I am not extravagant. I don't even have money to buy a pair of stockings.

S.M.: This was not projected. You might have felt a run in one of your stockings, for instance. If you had used the psychophysical steps in your inner monologue with expressive gestures we might have formed the idea that he does not give you enough money. This is only an example.

Next you will be a "thief in a dark room." Make sure you know what you are stealing and why. You may be starving and want a piece of bread, or you may want someone's jewelry or a document. Go on as soon as you have built the situation and remembered an analogous emotion. The situation does not have to be analogous; you do not have to be a burglar in your own life. Remember an analogous emotion: hunger, revenge, greed.

(*Mat performs the improvisation.*)
Were there any people in the house? Did you know this room?

Mat: I knew it fairly well. There was one person in the apartment, but definitely not nearby.

S.M.: All this might have influenced you. If there had been people around, you might have gone to the door first to make sure no one was near. You might also have barricaded the door with some furniture. You would have been overcoming obstacles to your objective. The psychophysical steps and the expressive gestures were missing.
(*Robert performs the improvisation.*)
Where were you?

Robert: I was in a room with a lot of antique books. I was tempted to steal a book with a leather binding. I smelled it. (*Laughter*)

S.M.: I did not understand why you smelled it.

Robert: Some antique books have a certain odor.

S.M.: All right. Did you take what you wanted? How can I impress on you that everything you do on stage must be understood by the spectators? All you have to do is build interesting content and find an interesting form to express it.

Mat: That's all? (*Laughter*)

S.M.: You remind me of something else. One director said at a conference that some actors will soon abolish the audience because they disturb their performance! Let us go on with the thief exercise.

(*Kathy performs the improvisation.*)

What was wrong with that?

Jim: First of all, in a dark room the tendency is not to squint as she was doing, but to open your eyes like this—as wide as possible. Also, after a certain period of time your eyes will have adjusted somewhat to the dark.

Kathy: If I am going to be in a blind situation, I shut my eyes and imagine how it would be. I try to feel how a blind person would feel.

S.M.: Why would you, as a blind person, run as you did? You knew exactly where you were going.

Kathy: I just ran into the corner.

S.M.: How did you know there was an empty corner?

Kathy: My first reaction was to get out of the center of the room.

S.M.: What kind of room was it?

Kathy: It was a room on the first floor of an abandoned house on Twenty-second Street in New York. My story was that I had seen a little bench there, and I wanted to

take it for my apartment. Even if I were breaking in at
night in complete darkness, I would have known roughly
where it was.

S.M.: You would not have to tell this interesting story if
you had found actions to express your circumstances. It
certainly is impossible to project a Twenty-second Street
address. Your rushing around proved that you forgot you
were in the dark, and it was not truthful. Please, keep
asking yourself, "What would I do IF? It is fantastic how
much this "IF" helps, especially because it helps you to
find what is personal to you.

Now we shall begin oral improvisations, because now
you have the idea of thinking on stage. With no words
to hide behind, you learned to think in silences. This is
an important step forward in your studies.

Words are verbal actions. Like all physical action,
verbal action is a means of expressing inner life. Work
on words is work on the inner world of the character and
on his relationship with the world that surrounds him.
The effect on the audience depends on what you put into
the words. The images in your words stirred by the
muscles of your body must stir images and associations
in the spectators. The great singer Feodor Chaliapin
made the spectators all but perspire with one word:
"Fire!" They say that Chaliapin's intonations were
flowing out of his body. When we speak in life, we are
trying to influence the emotions of the other person—
when, for example, you speak of something tragic. Words
are important but equally important are gestures of the
body and mise-en-scènes. As in life you must wonder
about and evaluate the other person, and watch him in

order to see whether you are achieving the expected results. Let us say you want to change the other person's mood. For instance, you are talking to a girl who is sad, and you want to cheer her up. While you are talking to her, you watch to see whether she smiles.

Now you will "persuade another person to do something you want him to do." Choose partners. You must know your motivation. It must be important to you. Know who you are to each other. Think of an analogous emotion in your own life. Your objective and the circumstances you build will tell you how to achieve your aim. Overcoming obstacles to your objective will influence your tempo-rhythm and give color to your actions. As in the silent improvisations, do not think of the *how* before you know the *why*, *where*, and so on. Try in every possible way to persuade your partner. Try to find conflicting text and subtext, i.e. contrast the words that you say and their real meaning. For instance, you may not like the person, but to persuade him you are trying to be especially nice to him. The subtext must be projected with gestures during silences. These ways, or adaptations, create the inner and physical communion on stage. If one way does not work, think of another. There must be a counteraction and a conflict in each improvisation. You must know what you want and why you want it, and the other person must know why he refuses. Use your muscles to stir wondering, evaluating, deciding, and gesturing before you begin the verbal action. You may speak only after you have carried out the psychophysical steps. After you have spoken, make another gesture and begin another action with the same steps.

John and Tom, go on stage. I shall give you the situation. John, you are talking Tom into robbing a bank. The situation does not have to be your own life situation. It is the analogous emotion in life that is important to remember. In the situation I gave you, you want a lot of money. In your life you might have wanted something else.

John: Does it have to be a bank?

S.M.: If you want it to be an individual who has enough money to satisfy you, that is all right.
(They perform the improvisation.)
Well, Tom, if you refuse, you must have a reason. Why didn't you want to take part in the robbery? You just kept saying, "No, I don't want to." Was that because you were an honest man, or simply because the job wasn't important enough? It was not clear at all. You were just talking. John was quite convincing in painting a beautiful future for you—the cruises and the beautiful women you could take along. But you expressed no attitude toward what he said nor your reasons for refusing. Still, for your first oral improvisation, it was not too bad.

I would like to see you put all this work to use in a scene from *The Three Sisters*. Let us see Joan and Tom do the scene between Irina and Soliony.

Soliony (Tom): Nobody here. Where are they all?

Irina (Joan): Gone home.

Soliony: That's strange. You're alone here.

Irina: Alone. *(Pause)* Good-bye—

S.M.: (*interrupting*) What are you writing, Irina?

Joan: I am copying from a book.

S.M.: That's wrong for this particular moment.

Joan: I was trying to get my mind off my troubles with the book and paper.

S.M.: You might try to concentrate on the book, but you look too busy. Irina does not know what to do with herself. Tom, is the argument you had with Andrei still on your mind when you enter this room?

Tom: Yes.

S.M.: Joan, you don't react at all when he asks, "Nobody here?" You look as if you were waiting for your cue. Don't you think that you should answer his question even if you have no lines to say? You do not know that he will say something else. Give him your right hand, not your left. Tom, your standing there upstage is too prolonged.

Tom: When she says good-bye, do you want me to start leaving?

S.M.: Yes. What you're doing is fine, but your moment of hesitation is too long. And Irina, you'll have to change your inner monologue and its expression, because the other actor didn't behave the way you expected. You must coordinate your behavior and his.

Soliony: Nobody here. Where are they all?

Irina: Gone home.

S.M.: Just a second. What you do, Tom, would be right for you or someone else, but not for Soliony. Soliony never bends. He thinks this is undignified. He has no experience in speaking of love. He is very stiff. He always looks like a soldier on guard. Joan, you want to get rid of him. But Irina is a lady, and she doesn't shout. Tom, justify your standing upstage. Is it because you do not dare look her in the eye? Let us start again.

> **Soliony**: Nobody here. Where are they all?
>
> **Irina**: Gone home.
>
> **Soliony**: That's strange. You're alone here.
>
> **Irina**: Alone. (*Pause*) Good-bye.
>
> **Soliony**: I behaved tactlessly just now. But you are not like the others, you are superior and pure, you see the truth. Only you can understand me. I love you deeply, endlessly.
>
> **Irina**: Good-bye! Go away.
>
> **Soliony**: I can't live without you. Oh, my heaven! Oh, happiness! Such magnificent, wonderful, marvelous eyes as I have never seen in any other woman. . . .
>
> **Irina**: Stop it, Vassili Vassilievitch!
>
> **Soliony**: It is the first time that I've spoken of love to you, and it is as if I were not on earth but on another planet. Well, it is all the same. You can't force anyone to love you, of course. But I can't have lucky rivals, there must not be. . . . I swear to you by all that's holy, I'll kill any rival. . . . Oh, wonderful one!

S.M.: There has been definite progress. When you started, you were just coming out of a blue sky every time you said a word. It ended much better, but still vague. Your gestures could be more expressive.

When I see your discouraged faces, I can't help thinking of what happened to the Habima Theatre. After the leaders of that group talked with Stanislavski, they told their actors, "We must close our theatre and study." Most of the actors were disappointed and left, but those who remained built one of the best theatres in Moscow. I wish Stanislavski could talk to our actors.

Soliony, you are standing there without any reaction to Irina.

Kathy: (*interrupting*) Only now do I know what it means to react to each other on stage. I have been told for years that I must react, but no one ever explained how.

S.M.: Some people think that ensemble will be achieved when we have repertory theatres and people work together for years. Well, I saw some actors who had such good fortune, but there was no hint of an ensemble at work in their performances. It is when the expression of one person's face changes the expression of another that you can call it ensemble work. Without this technique ensemble work will never exist, no matter how long a group of actors perform together. Ensemble is the actors' inner and external reactions to one another in a mutual endeavor to project the superobjective of a play.

Now you, Irina—

Joan: (*interrupting*) I came downstairs because I had nothing to do, so I just sat down.

S.M.: All right, but didn't you hear Soliony's footsteps?

Joan: I heard footsteps, but I thought they might have been Natasha's.

S.M.: Would Natasha's steps sound like Soliony's? Natasha does not walk. She flits around like a butterfly. Even if you thought it was Natasha, wouldn't you react in some way? And here all of a sudden Soliony appears. You did not know he was still in the house, and yet you don't react at all. This is what I was trying to make you understand with the oral improvisations and earlier in the silent improvisations when there was more than one of you on stage. You must watch each other, sense each other, hear and see each other. Every role depends on all roles. You must know what the other one is doing because your own behavior depends on it. You must react to Soliony's entrance. I don't mean you should jump, but you should wonder, evaluate and make decisions.

Tom: When I wonder and evaluate, should I look at her or away?

S.M.: Tom, I don't want to tell you everything. You have an idea what a psychophysical action is. What do you think would be the logical thing to do?

Your standing upstage for such a long time looks unjustified, but I agree you should be upstage. Think more about it, and find the justification. Also, when you threaten "I'll kill any rival," it must be more convincing. Before and after the words use a meaningful gesture to project what the words cannot project.

I want the audience to wonder why Irina does not take this more seriously. If she did, she might have prevented Tusenbach's death. Soliony is dangerous because he senses his inferiority. Such people may try to destroy those they consider superior. It is tragic that none of these nice people understands Soliony. They simply witness the tragedy.

Sharon: Mrs. Moore, as I told you, I may have to leave the Studio in February. Will I have learned by then how to build a character? Or will you start working on building the character next semester? You know, I would like to be a director.

S.M.: We have already started the work on building the character. Purposeful physical actions, emotions, images, and inner monologues are essential steps in the process. But, of course, you will not have learned to build a character by February. You will have learned a great deal, but there will be much more.

Sharon: After this term, I mean after the sixteen weeks, will there be anything new to learn?

S.M.: There will be something new all the time.

Sharon: You mean, I will not learn it all before I leave?

S.M.: Do you expect to learn your profession in sixteen weeks?

Sharon: Oh, that's terribly discouraging.

S.M.: After sixteen weeks you will understand a great deal. You will have assimilated some of the technique. But after sixteen weeks of studying dance, you would not be able to dance a solo.

■ Class Nine

Kathy: Mrs. Moore, in the last class you asked us to find conflicting text and subtext. I should know what subtext is by now—but every time I think I've got a grip on it, it kind of slips away.

SONIA MOORE: It's the sign of a professional to admit ignorance. Some actors have gone through their entire careers without dispelling the mystery around the subtext. You still have your whole career ahead of you. Let us start by giving you some background. The term "subtext" arose during the Moscow Art Theatre productions of Chekhov's plays. It was used to help an actor understand the full meaning of a character's speech. Stanislavski and Nemirovich-Danchenko found in subtext a means to discover and express ever-more-subtle nuances of emotion and thought. It became a vital instrument of an actor's conscious creativity.

Subtext does not only refer to what underlies the words a character speaks. Stanislavski and Nemirovich-Danchenko also proposed a subtext of behavior that refers to what a person means by his actions. Subtext influences everything that is spoken or done. It is the interpretation of behavior, the significance of the objects that serve as motivation. The subtext of words is only a part of the character's inner life.

For actors, the subtext is a means both for analyzing a character and for making the behavior of the character clear to the audience. When an actor understands the character's subtext, he will have assimilated the profound causes and inner reasons for his stage actions. Understanding a character's subtext will help an actor choose actions that are necessary and clear to the audience.

In order to understand the subtext, actors and directors must study the play and the relationships of the characters. They must depart from the superobjective and the through line of actions and study each character's particular inner world. When an actor has a profound understanding of the character's motivations and attitudes, only then will he have assimilated the subtext.

Find a subtext that conflicts with the text. There must be a collision between a character's real strivings and what he actually says or does. A startling contrast between what a character thinks and what he says creates drama in each actor's performance. Contradiction between the text and the subtext makes the word unexpected, vivid, and significant. The subtext must be strong, the needs and desires it expresses important to the character.

Subtext makes a word unique, its meaning unrepeatable. It helps an actor transform a word or line into verbal action by providing the justification, the inner need, for its expression. Different subtexts give the same words different sounds. According to Stanislavski, "The value of words is not in the words themselves but in the subtext they contain. The meaning of stage creativity is in subtext, without which words have nothing to do on stage."

Work on the subtext begins with memorizing lines

as soon as possible. Stanislavski and Nemirovich-Danchenko argued about this. Today Russian theatre scholars agree with Nemirovich-Danchenko: lines must be learned by the actor from the very beginning. I agree with them. Before an actor can understand and make a dramatist's language, style and unique diction his own, the lines must first be memorized. Even if an actor understands a character's actions and motivations, without the text he will not be able to understand fully the subtext or its relationship to the text.

To express the subtext the actor must be capable of executing a psychophysical action. The expression of the subtext through nonverbal means must be sharp; it must reach the actor's fellow actors and the audience. Expressed subtext gives the audience unexpected knowledge of a character and reveals the essence of his behavior.

The subtext can be expressed through physical means: body gestures, glances, the use of props. Actors can also express subtext by changing their tempo-rhythm. Physical expression of a subtext that conflicts with the text builds dramatic and comic effects. This also avoids illustrating the text with gestures and movements; actors should not use their body to repeat their words' meaning.

Although in life we often do not reveal our subtext, in theatre it should always be projected. It must be continuously incarnated in visual signs. Without subtext there is no theatre, said Stanislavski.

Now, before proceeding with the exercises, I want to know what scenes you want to do next. We have been working on *The Three Sisters*. We must now take another step. I want to see other scenes. But do not abandon *The*

Three Sisters until you have actually begun working on a scene from another play.

Joan: May I work on *Blood Wedding*?

S.M.: Garcia Lorca is one of my favorite dramatists and his writing is pure poetry, but at this stage of your studies I would prefer something in simple language. I do not think you will be able to do thorough work on it. Lorca's clarity is often subordinated to the musicality of verse. Keep it in mind for your next scene. How about working on Abigail in Arthur Miller's *The Crucible*?

Joan: Oh, I would love it.

Sharon: May I also work on Abigail?

S.M.: Good. I like to see several people working on the same scene. You learn a great deal by watching others. And John, I think you should work on John Proctor. Chris and Maria, how about a scene from *Another Part of the Forest*? Do you know the play?

Chris: By Lillian Hellman. Yes.

S.M.: Begin your work on new scenes by reading the play as many times as you can. Regina and Ben are ready to cut each other's throats for money. You must build characters who will be symbols of greed. We should try to project such a phenomenon through those people. You must penetrate to its roots. Is it nourished by life in the South? Ask yourself what you want to project; what kind of atmosphere will surround you? After you have studied the play, write your character's biography, as you did in *The Three Sisters*. What is your character striving for? What is his superobjective? Improvise on his past.

Analyze your particular scene. If the scene is one event give it a name—a noun—that will characterize the scene. If there are different important episodes in the scene, each one must have a characteristic name. In our improvisations, you either built a situation or assumed the situation I gave you. In a play the author gives you the circumstances. An important event, or an episode, must have a characteristic name. For instance, if you call a moment on stage "war," this will dictate certain behavior to you. Decide on the main objective of the scene; only then can you begin analyzing actions.

Kathy: How about images and inner monologues?

S.M.: They are essential parts of psychophysical action. The inner monologue is most important because it continues the flow of action onstage during silences. But since we know that words do not always incarnate our thoughts, the inner monologue is not fluid; it is condensed, broken up. In life we rarely say what we think. Search for contrast between what has to be projected and the words which can only partially express it. The inner monologue and an expressive body must project the subtext through the silences. Inner experiences must reach the audience before it hears the words.

When you find names for the events and choose your actions, you have begun to use Stanislavski's analysis of the play through events and actions. This includes finding the superobjective and the through line of actions—the chain of logical, typical, consecutive actions that will gradually disclose the superobjective. It will also give you a clearer idea of your character's super-objective.

Coordinate your preparation with your partner. You must understand your partner's actions and write them down as well as your own. Perform as many improvisations as possible on the situations in the play. Speculate on credible events not in the play. Reread the play and the scene you are working on. Follow the actions in your mind. Avoid playing the result in your improvisations. Fight the temptation to do superficial work; it will only result in cliché.

Before we begin blocking the scene, memorize your lines. Show the scene to me. We shall continue to work on it together until we have brought it into the best possible shape. We must select the best means to express the character's contribution to the play. Remember that each scene must have a beginning, i.e. exposition, a development, and a conclusion.

Chris: How do I determine an action? Do I use my own judgment?

S.M.: First study the play. You choose an action to achieve an objective. Improvisations on an action will help you determine whether the action is the right one. Remember that an action is an act of human behavior, a union of thoughts and emotions, within a series of purposeful physical movements.

And now let us proceed with our improvisations. This chair is a vicious dog. He is on a chain, but he can reach and tear you to shreds. For some reason of your own, you must cross the yard. The reason should be important. For instance, you may be a doctor bringing medicine to a dying patient. Do not try to believe that the chair is really a dog. Build the circumstances and then choose your actions, or what you would do in life in such a situation. You must treat the chair *as if it were* a dog; do not force yourself to see a dog there. Is that clear? It is what you do that will make us believe that you are trying to avoid a dog. Concentrate and build the imaginary circumstances.

(*All the students perform the improvisation.*)

Good. Mat, I like your idea of using a hamburger to distract the dog, as Jerry did in *The Zoo Story*.

Now this chair is a throne. You must build the situation and treat this plain old chair in such a way that we will believe that it is a throne.

Dan: In a play this would be much easier because of the sets and the right props.

S.M.: Yes, in most cases. The audience would see a throne, but even then you would have to treat it as one.

John: Must we be a king or a queen?

S.M.: Not necessarily. Build the circumstances in which you would be in a room where there is a throne. Ready?

(*Students perform the improvisation.*)

Dan, if you know where you are, we would like to know, too!

Dan: You mean you must know what country I am in?

S.M.: No. We do not have any idea that it is a throne.

John: Are you a king?

Dan: I was a king in the nineteenth century. It is very difficult to project.

S.M.: It is doubtful that in the nineteenth century a king would sit on a throne doing nothing. I am sure that such a king would sit on an ordinary chair when he signed papers. A king might sit on his throne when he made a declaration or received ambassadors.

Dan: I was honest—I believed and I fulfilled what I believed.

S.M.: Oh, it is always I, I, I! You must realize that there is no place for you on stage unless you are capable of projecting what is taking place. The audience must be affected by what you are doing. Otherwise stay in your room and "feel" and "believe" for your own enjoyment.

(Sharon performs the improvisation.)

That was very good, Sharon. It was clear that you were in a church. I saw you in St. Peter's in Rome. According to Stanislavski, the only things that an actor can do honestly are simple physical actions, which are miraculously expressive. Sharon took some water, and made the sign of the cross, and went down on her knees. She used the muscles around her spine and fulfilled very simple actions that could be performed easily and truthfully by any actor. And they were not indications.

And now the same chair is an electric chair.

John: Do we die in it or . . .

S.M.: It depends on what situation you want to build. Build the circumstances.

(*The students perform the improvisation.*)

Very good, Tom. At first I expected you to be executed in this chair.

Tom: No, I was a guard checking the wiring.

S.M.: Yes, you made that clear afterward. Kathy, you made clear that you were in some sinister museum, and that you wanted to touch the chair but did not dare. Your wondering, evaluating, and making decisions and the gestures were clear. Well, don't you think we are improving and our imaginations have developed quite well?

Let us perform an oral improvisation on an action "to make another person leave."

Mat: Get rid of someone?

S.M.: Yes, but not physically. Talk over the situation with your partner—decide who you are to each other, but do not tell your partner why you want him to leave. Your partner should not say how he will react. I want this to be unexpected for each of you. When you realize that he wants you to leave, react accordingly—the way you would in a situation in life. Remember an analogous emotion in your life. Briefly discuss the situation with each other. Make sure you watch each other carefully. Wonder, evaluate, and make decisions.

(*Improvisation. After speaking a great deal about how much work he has to do, John tells Mat that he has a headache and takes a pill. Mat at last is convinced and leaves. Then John rushes to the phone.*)

That was good. John projected irritation because Mat would not leave, but tried to be nice to him. There was conflicting text and subtext. Do you understand that I gave you the physical side of the action? "To make another person leave" is the physical action. The psychological side is your reason for wanting him to leave as well as images of people, places, and events in your mind. You must add the psychological side. After you have done this, go on stage to fulfill the physical action "to make him leave."

John: Mrs. Moore, we have a surprise for you. Ruth and I have been working on the scene between Irina and Tusenbach in the first act of *The Three Sisters*. May we show it to you?

S.M.: I'd be delighted.

> **Irina (Ruth)**: Masha is in a bad mood today. She married when she was eighteen, and he seemed to her the most intelligent man in the world. But now it's different. He is the kindest man but not the most intelligent.
>
> **Tusenbach (John)**: What are you thinking about?

Irina: Well, I dislike and fear that Soliony of yours. He says only stupid things.

Tusenbach: He is a strange man. I feel sorry for him and annoyed, but mostly sorry. It seems to me that he's shy. . . . When there are only the two of us, he's sometimes very clever and kind, but in company he's rude, a rabid duelist. Don't go. Let them sit down at the table. Let me be near you a while. What are you thinking about? (*Pause*) You're twenty years old and I'm not yet thirty. How many years we have ahead, a long, long row of days, filled with my love for you. . . .

Irina: Nikolai Lvovich, don't talk to me about love.

Tusenbach: (*Not listening*) I have a passionate thirst for life, struggle, hard work, and this thirst in my soul has merged with my love for you, Irina, and it is as if you are beautiful by some design, and life seems to me so beautiful! What are you thinking about?

Irina: You say life is beautiful. But what if it only seems to be? With us, the three sisters, life is not yet beautiful; it stifles us as grass is by weeds. I'm crying—I shouldn't. We must work, work. We are bored and have such gloomy outlook on life because we don't know labor. We were born of people who despised work.

S.M.: You have objectives, actions, images. You wonder, evaluate, and make decisions. Your body is expressive.

But—and I'm sorry to disappoint you—your actions are wrong for Irina and Tusenbach. You have built totally different characters. You have built a Soliony rather than a Tusenbach—and Ruth, Irina would never be rude to Tusenbach. She likes him very much. Everyone likes the noble friend. John, Tusenbach does not know that Irina doesn't love him. He is so in love with her and he is such an enthusiast that he does not hear her until the fourth act, when she says that she will be a faithful wife to him but cannot love him. This is just before Tusenbach goes to the duel with Soliony. This is what kills him before he is actually killed in the duel.

Your impression of these people is wrong. You must change your objectives, your actions and your images; you must find and move other muscles.

Also, everyone, it is time for you to pay more attention to the words you speak. Different words have different values. Do not swallow the ends of words. Choose ones that you think are important and emphasize them. For example, "Tomorrow is Friday. I don't *have* to attend, but I'll go *anyway*. . . . It is boring *at home*. . . . How *strangely* life changes and *deceives us*."

You should start working on a new scene as soon as possible without discarding the one you have been working on. This scene should serve as an example for further work.

John: Mrs. Moore, when I start to work on *The Crucible*, do I start working on images and the inner monologue first, or on actions?

S.M.: On actions, actions! The inner monologue and images are part of the action. But first you must understand the play. Write a biography of John Proctor. Then think of what Proctor's superobjective is.

John: You mean in a scene?

S.M.: First his superobjective in the whole play and then in your scene.

John: I thought I'd start by working on images.

S.M.: This is wrong, John. The circumstances, your objectives, and your actions will suggest the right images to you. Do you know what the scene is about? You must know what you have to project. Find the name for the scene. In this case the scene is one event. This event will dictate your actions to you. The action will suggest your images.

John: May we show you next time at least a little bit of it?

S.M.: Yes, but first do some more preparatory work. I would rather see it before you become so proud of your magnificent work that you will resist criticism. And read other works by Arthur Miller. Read everything you can about the dramatist. Understand his way of thinking.

■ Class Ten

SONIA MOORE: We are about to perform a difficult exercise. I shall ask you questions and you must respond without hesitation. First take it in, wonder, evaluate, make a quick decision, and make a gesture before and after you speak. The answer must be logical. This is another way to "massage" your mind. You need an alert, fertile imagination. Kathy, somebody told me they saw you with a baby in your arms, near Park Avenue and Fifty-third Street, at five in the morning. What were you doing there?

Kathy: It was my friend's baby.

S.M.: But why at five o'clock in the morning?

Kathy: Well, there was some trouble with burglars and I had to—

S.M.: The police took the baby away, and they told me that you began to run

Kathy: Yes, yes. I remembered that Mother was going to call from Canada and I had to be home.

S.M.: And Joan, I saw you with an old gentleman yesterday at eleven in the morning. Who was he?

Joan: An old gentleman?

S.M.: Don't stall for time. Answer right away, but first move your muscles to stir mental processes. And don't forget the gestures. Make sure they are meaningful. Your inner experiences must reach the audience before you say a single word.

Joan: Oh, he fell, and I was taking him home.

S.M.: Why did you run?

Joan: I saw a taxi and ran after it.

S.M.: But when a taxi stopped you refused to get in. You called a policeman instead. Why?

Joan: Why did I? (*Laughter*) Oh, because the old man started to become nasty.

S.M.: And that is why you went into a bar?

Joan: Well, I needed a drink.

S.M.: Mat, I saw a young woman waving to you, and you hid around the corner, and she started to scream for help.

Mat: I threw my coat over my head, and she thought I was a gangster or something.

S.M.: Maria, where were you going last night with that nice young man?

Maria: We went to a movie.

S.M.: Which one?

Maria: *Citizen Kane.*

S.M.: But you came out right away.

Maria: We were hungry.

S.M.: In the restaurant, so they told me, you threw your glass at him.

Maria: Yes, well, we had a fight. We fight a lot, and we'd just had another.

S.M.: Debbi, what were you doing at Bloomingdale's this morning?

Debbi: Buying a hat.

S.M.: How much did you pay?

Debbi: Two ninety-eight. It was on sale.

S.M.: They stopped you at the door to check whether you had paid for it.

Debbi: There was some shoplifting in another part of

the store, and they asked me for the receipt.

S.M.: Why did you scream then?

Debbi: That was someone else, not me.

S.M.: And why did you go into the telephone booth?

Debbi: I had to let a friend know I would be late for an appointment.

S.M.: Oh, but then you came out before you even started to talk.

Debbi: No, I was talking, but my friend started yelling that I am always late, so I hung up.

S.M.: Robert, who was the girl you were walking with near the Four Seasons?

Robert: Near what?

S.M.: A restaurant, the Four Seasons. Who was the young girl?

Robert: A girlfriend.

S.M.: What is her name?

Robert: Olga.

S.M.: Why were you there at six in the morning?

Robert: Well, we like fresh air. (*Laughter*)

S.M.: Why were you arguing?

Robert: Well, she did not want to get up at five in the morning, but I said, "If you want to get out by six, you have to get up by five." (*Laughter*)

S.M.: Sharon, I saw you in a restaurant with a middle-aged gentleman with glasses. Who was he?

Sharon: Who was he? (*Laughter*)

S.M.: Answer—no stalling!

Sharon: I am wondering. (*Laughter*) He was a man from a film company.

S.M.: He did not behave very nicely.

Sharon: What happened?

S.M.: He threw a bottle at somebody. It seems that I am answering your questions!

Sharon: Oh, I insulted him.

S.M.: What happened?

Sharon: I told him he made second-rate films.

S.M.: So he threw a bottle at the bartender?

Sharon: He missed me, I ducked.

S.M.: Pat, I saw you with a young man at ten in the morning. First you kissed each other, and then you slapped him. What was the matter?

Pat: Well, you know how it is . . . (*Laughter*) It is a very personal thing, and he started to be extremely fresh.

S.M.: Did you know that they took him to the police station?

Pat: Oh, I am delighted to hear that.

S.M.: Did they let him out?

Pat: Well, yes. They let him out. It was all a case of mistaken identity. Somebody had stolen a dog, apparently an expensive French poodle, and they thought he was the man.

S.M.: When they let him out, where did you go with him?

Pat: We went to this crazy pub where they have German beer.

S.M.: Chris, take over. As soon as you entered the pub, someone asked you to come out again.

Chris: That was my mother.

S.M.: Where did you go?

Chris: She wanted me to catch a cab and come straight home. She did not approve of the girl I was with. (*Laughter*)

S.M.: Were you aware that you were wondering and evaluating because you were yourself? Well, that is enough. (*Students express relief.*)
Next, we will "eavesdrop." Know your objective. Build the circumstances. Why you eavesdrop, where, when, all the possible details.
(*Dan performs the improvisation.*)
You said you were in an agent's office? How do we know that?

Dan: But this is terribly difficult.

S.M.: Yes, it is. Give it a thought. After all, we are your audience. We don't know where you are, what you are doing there . . .

Dan: I am just sitting and smoking in an agent's office.

S.M.: You must know that on stage nothing can be "just." You can also sit and smoke in a doctor's office. Why did you come here? Did the agent call you and tell you that there was a leading part for you in a movie? Or is this the first time you have been in an agent's office? (*Silence*) Well, what do you think was wrong, Tom?

Tom: His physical actions did not express anything.

Maria: His tempo-rhythm was wrong.

S.M.: Right. In life we do not have to think whether we should move faster or slower; we adjust spontaneously. You were *only* thinking. It was dead because you must function psychophysically to be alive. Even in your body-movement class you must think of psychophysical action. Think of it in your dance class, and your speech class, too.

There should be no movement or word without an objective, concrete circumstances, images, and a subtext. Exercise your imagination and put life in your movements. All the great dancers do this. They use their movements to express inner content. In every art the most important goal is spiritual content expressed in an artistic form. A good portrait breathes life. You can see life in the faces and the hands. The same principle applies to music. Some musicians are extraordinary. It is difficult for me to keep up with their images. And yesterday I heard a violinist—some people say he is very good. Perhaps he is a great technician, but to me he seemed dead. In this studio, whatever you do, there must be inner content expressed in laconic, eloquent form.

Who is next to "eavesdrop"?

(Mat performs the improvisation. He sits and types, then stops, puzzling over the paper in the typewriter. He gets up and goes to a closed door, pauses, and moves nearer to listen.)

Good. You established that you were in an office. You had to ask your boss about something. There was someone with him, and you became interested in their conversation. You were wondering, evaluating, making decisions and meaningful gestures; it was all clear. Who is next please?

(*John performs the improvisation.*)

S.M.: What did the audience understand?

Ruth: He had his blood taken for analysis and naturally wanted to know what they were discussing in the doctor's office.

S.M.: When you looked under your bandage, it was more than a mechanical movement because you were wondering and evaluating; your muscular movements were right and your eyes were alive.
(*Everyone performs the improvisation.*)
You see how different all of you were at eavesdropping? No two of you behaved the same way. First, because you each had different circumstances and second, because you are all different people. Every character has a different psychological and a different physical behavior.

Three people on stage, please. Mat and Pat, you are spies, and one of you must pass an important document to the other spy. Ruth, you are a detective, and you are at the place where the spies meet. Build your circumstances. Know whom you are spying for. To be caught may mean life imprisonment or death.

Mat: Do we know that she is a detective?

S.M.: No, but you would not dare pass the document in anybody's presence, spy or not.

(*Improvisation*)

Well, spies with an important document would probably pretend not to know each other in the presence of a third person. Your behavior would attract anyone's attention, not only a detective's. This is an improvisation in *communion* on stage, without speaking. You must catch each other's glances, each other's movements. And the detective should not alert them that he is watching.

Mat: We were at the bus terminal, and there were other people around. You couldn't get away with false pretenses like reading a magazine.

S.M.: We did not believe that you were aware of the danger you were in. Am I right? Two spies seeing another person, especially someone behaving as suspiciously as Ruth did, would not sit next to each other. I want you to sense each other, to catch each other's looks, barely perceptible signs, which the detective would not discern. Maybe you could put the document where the detective would never suspect you could have put it. You did not think of your physical state. It would have influenced the tempo-rhythm, and a special atmosphere would have been created.

Mat: Couldn't I have put it in her pocket as I did?

Ruth: Oh, I thought you put it under the chair!

S.M.: A real detective would have seen where he put it. Don't you think so?

Ruth: Yes, I do.

Pat: I thought that the obvious thing for us to do was to pretend that we were not afraid and thus fool her.

S.M.: Suppose that Mat is a dangerous spy and his face is known to the FBI. Would you have wanted to be seen with him? I want you to be some distance away from each other so that you must attract each other's attention with glances or barely perceptible signs. Action is not enough. You must select the *right* actions.

Let us proceed with an oral improvisation. The action is "to encourage." Choose your partner and decide on your objective. Know the circumstances. Think of an emotion that should be stirred in this situation and remember an analogous emotion in life. Do not rush; the more circumstances you bring into the picture, the more interesting your actions will be.

If your partner lets himself be encouraged right away, then you will not have to make any effort—and the action will never be fully explored. Your partner must create obstacles. His resistance will create a conflict. Everything depends on the circumstances you build. What would you do in such a situation in your life? Never forget the "magic IF." Concentrate. The means to be used will depend on the other person's reaction. In life, we try one way, and if it does not work, we try another, more persuasive way. Look for contrasting text and subtext.

(*All the students perform the improvisation.*)

Joan: Mrs. Moore, I have started working on *The Crucible* scene. I was wondering whether we should give one name to the whole scene or divide it into several units?

S.M.: If the whole scene is one event, one episode, don't subdivide it. But your actions may change a great deal in the course of the same event. Did you think about the superobjective of the character you will portray? What is the scene about? What has to be projected in it? Though it is a short scene, we should treat it as a whole play. We must always remember Arthur Miller's super-objective. Joan?

Joan: A confrontation between two people who are attracted to each other, but finally Proctor's decency takes over.

S.M.: Do you agree, John?

John: Yes, but also the idea that no matter how involved a man is with someone, he can still be good.

S.M.: What name have you given to the scene?

John: "The meeting of two people attracted to each other."

S.M.: Could you think of one word for it?

Joan: Could it be "pitfall"?

S.M.: Let us see. You both agree that Proctor and Abigail are attracted to each other. Let us start from the beginning. What is your first action?

John: To wait for Abigail.

S.M.: Fine, but you can wait for different reasons, with different objectives, and in different circumstances. And since you consider this event a pitfall, as soon as you enter we must know that Proctor is waiting in the circumstances of a pitfall. Also, you must make us understand that this is a forest, that it is night, and that you are not eager to be seen. These are also your circumstances, which have to be projected. We must create atmosphere. From the moment the curtain goes up the spectators must understand what is taking place at that moment.

John: Oh, I'll have to change everything I thought I would do.

S.M.: Of course. You did not expect to have everything right before we'd even started! The Stanislavski System gives us unlimited possibilities to change and grow. The more deeply we analyze the events and the actions, the more the essence of the play will be brought to the surface. You must understand the play thoroughly to convey it to the audience. You should also know what attracted you to this play, what your super-superobjective is, i.e., what you wish to contribute with your work. Did you read the play again before you wrote your biography?

John: Yes, and I saw things I hadn't noticed before.

S.M.: I am sure of that. And if you read it again, you will see more. Writing a biography forces you to read and study the play. You cannot depend only on me; and you must argue with me if you think that I am wrong. You must learn to work independently. Both of you realize that Arthur Miller is a dramatist with strong convictions.

You know that Proctor is a good man. You also told me, John, that Proctor was afraid of his attraction to Abigail, and that is why he had postponed seeing her in order to persuade her to stop the horror.

John: Right.

S.M.: All this has to be projected. We study the play a second time and write the biography with the sole purpose of learning about the character and to be able to build him.

Chris: I read *Another Part of the Forest* three times, and I think I know what Lillian Hellman wants to say. What horrible characters.

S.M.: What about you, Kathy?

Kathy: I am in the middle of my third reading, but I wrote the biography.

Chris: I wrote the biography of Ben after I read it twice, but when I began to read the play a third time I made a lot of changes.

Kathy: Yes, I changed it, too.

S.M.: Good. what else did you do?

Chris: Kathy and I met, and we lost a lot of time trying to decide on the name for the scene.

S.M.: I don't agree that you were losing time. A word that will tell you clearly what the whole scene is about is of great help, because then you know what the audience must understand. Disclosing the essence of an event is the gradual disclosing of the play's theme. You achieve this with actions dictated by the event. Eugene Vakhtangov said, "A unit in a role or scene is a step in moving the through line of actions toward the goal," or the superobjective. You must start improvisations on the past of the characters.

You have done enough work now to begin moving, improvising on stage. When you have learned the analysis through events and actions, and how to use the given circumstances, you will not waste time on long discussions. Analysis through actions must be done with all the psychic and physical forces of an actor. Achieving psychophysical unity in a given situation is the purpose of the whole Stanislavski technique. With the Method of Physical Actions, we analyze the role and the play *in action.*

What name did you give the scene?

Chris: We decided that it is "greed." Then Kathy and I worked on actions.

Kathy: We also worked on our inner monologues and images, but not very much.

S.M.: That is understandable. You cannot do it all in such a short time, but I am delighted that you started your work on a scene in the proper way. Let us stop talking and see the scene.

(*Scene*)

Yes, I realize that you did not have enough time to do thorough work. But one thing upsets me. We talked and talked about the play; you decided on the name for the scene; you wrote biographies; you said you knew the main objectives of your characters; you said that you searched for your actions, i.e., that you improvised on actions. But where is all this? It seems to me that the analysis you did, the study of the characters, the biography, and the rest, is only academic work for you.

This work has only one purpose: to project what you have learned about the play to the audience. Stanislavski said, "An actor becomes an actor when he masters the choice of actions." Nothing you did, not one of your actions—and I must say this to both of you—proves that you really searched for expressive actions. But to be frank, this should have been expected. To understand the System theoretically is one thing, but to make it work is another.

Unless you *assimilate* the technique, you don't really understand it. If you did assimilate the technique you would already be accomplished actors. When you have learned the artistic process of the choice of actions, you do not have to come here to study, only to practice. I am not joking. When this is taught in all drama schools and in all drama departments of our universities, there will be an acting profession in the United States. Now the majority of actors are only people who have made up their minds that they are actors. Real actors are those who can build characters in a play with their own psychophysical resources.

To assist you in analyzing the work of your fellow

artists, I have prepared a list of criteria by which all performances should be judged.

CRITERIA

Use the following to analyze the work of an actor or director. Do you see:

- An important event.
- An important superobjective.
- Given circumstances.
- Logical actions leading to achievement of the superobjective.
- The experience of an emotion.
- Sharp conflicts.
- Clear relationships.
- A subtext of behavior revealed by nonverbal means, i.e. through body gestures, the use of props, etc.
- Significant gestures contributing to the revelation of content.
- The achievement of psychophysical involvement when all the elements of an action (i.e. an act of human behavior) are present: relaxation, concentration, imagination, communion, tempo-rhythm, truth and belief, sense memory, and emotional memory.
- The actors reacting to each other and to everything on stage in a psychophysical way.
- The contribution of sets, lights, and music to the emotional content of the action on stage.

■ Class Eleven
The Director

*Even if you place a diamond into the mechanism, the watch
will stop. The stage does not bear anything superfluous,
anything that does not serve the intent, anything that does
not work for the superobjective. The stage demands absolute
precision: every second in time, and each half-inch of space
must be strictly considered. Even if only one role is outside
the unity, it will uproot the whole edifice of the performance,
violate its symphonic process.*

—A.D. Dyki, Soviet director

SONIA MOORE: Directing is a fascinating profession,
though perhaps at times unappreciated and a source of
torment and anxiety. A director has many moments of
frustration and doubt.

Every new production is an experiment because the
artist strives for the new, for the unique, for the never-
said-before. To find the harmonious relationship of
content and form is a gigantic problem with each new
production. Not every experiment succeeds. Geniuses
have erred and failed throughout history. Wagner's and
Mussorgsky's innovations were not recognized immediately, and yet they influenced opera throughout the
world. Only those who do not strive for the new, those
who are content to repeat their clichés over and over, do

not make mistakes and do not fail. They do not make discoveries either. These are tradesmen, not artists. Goethe said, "Every artist has in him the potentiality for daring; without it, talent is inconceivable."

The road toward creation of an original production is difficult for the director who is striving to express the idea of the work in the best possible way, better, perhaps, than the playwright himself expressed it. The director is really competing with the author in his search for the most expressive form for the content. Although the director has no right to distort the play, he is not obligated to express himself only *for* the author. He must express himself *through* the playwright. After listening to Chaliapin reading Alexander Pushkin's *Mozart and Salieri*, Stanislavski said, "A talent like Chaliapin takes Pushkin into his service, and one without such talent goes into Pushkin's service."

The professional acting technique that you have been mastering will be of great assistance to you as directors, because it enables you to help the actor. You will be able to live every moment of the actor's role and will be capable of offering suggestions that matter. As important as the technique is for directors, it alone is not sufficient. The level of your culture is also important in your work. Leo Tolstoy said, "Without ceasing to be a human being, one must also be an expert; expertise excludes dilettantism, and to be a dilettante means to be helpless."

Let me give you an idea what Meyerhold, the rebel, who fought everything that was dead in the theatre, thought of the significance of culture for directors. When Meyerhold was asked to write a guide for directing, he refused, saying, "It won't pay! It will be only a tiny booklet." Meyerhold believed that there were only a few rules for directing, that they could be described very briefly, and that not everyone was capable of understanding them. He thought that only a person of superior erudition and musicality would be able to use these laws in practice. Meyerhold demanded from his student directors a knowledge of every facet of the theatre. He saw the art of the director as a strict and precise mastership, spiritualized by poetry and fantasy. He detested those who knew how to patch up a performance. Meyerhold believed that in addition to poetry in art, there must be calculation—"arithmetic"—intellect, and boldness. His motto in directing was: "The revelation of human destiny with brilliant theatrical effect." When he succeeded in both, the result was overwhelming.

Meyerhold insisted that his students frequent libraries, concerts, art galleries, and museums. "You will not develop your taste by window shopping," said the master. "Think of Michelangelo, who was a painter, sculptor, and poet; he wrote sonnets, and when he had to, he could be a soldier."

Some young future directors, among them the celebrated Georgi Tovstonogov, came to Meyerhold for advice. He said, "You must go to museums continually, not only when you are staging a production. And don't read any reviews of a previous production while your idea about the play is still maturing. Read them when you are ready to begin staging the play. When your intent has matured, then read the reviews and go again to the museums. This will strengthen your intent. Use every opportunity to see paintings, even if only reproductions. Listen to symphonies as often as you can. Imitation of others is an almost obligatory stage in the formation of the artist. Beethoven began by imitating Mozart, Stanislavski by imitating Meiningen. The more original the master, the more difficult it is to free yourself from his influence." Meyerhold was a man of great culture. His education included architecture, painting, and literature. He was capable of detecting the slightest error in music.

Meyerhold demanded that the actor follow the director's score; a slight deviation from this precisely calculated score, he believed, leads to a violation of the composition as a whole. Meyerhold did not mean that actors have no right to say what they think. The director should listen to the actor's suggestions. Unfortunately the freedom given to actors often verges on dilettantism and leads to chaos. The director must surmount this chaos through artistic discipline, determined by his understanding of the objective and by his degree of aesthetic sensitivity.

One's capacity for feeling, for understanding and analyzing the times, depends on the progress of one's personal culture. As the director you will organize the creative process and define the relationships among the actors.

When choosing the repertory, the director should be able to understand life's social and psychological phenomena. The director must be capable of perception and sharp analysis. He must have sound logic. The director must foresee all the factors that influence the aesthetic perception of the spectators. The audience should not be treated lightly. The director is responsible for the ideals of his theatre; he must take a stand. Theatre that has no ideals will please people who have no taste. The lack of an ideological and artistic stand will result in a chaotic and worthless repertory. We can reach the spectators with the most profound thoughts in the form of entertainment and can help the actor to transform the spectators into his friends and make them think in unison with him. Our spectators should leave the theatre spiritually nourished. We cannot allow trivialities on stage.

Truth and oversimplification have often been equated. Truth is not always simple. In pursuit of external truthfulness, one may be apprehensive about using daring and original forms, but the expression of truth will be undermined by both artificiality and inexpressive naturalism. Without sincerity, true simplicity, and truthfulness, theatre will not stir the audience. But neither will theatre achieve these goals without expressive form.

Strong emotions and fierce inner conflicts must have external expression in space, in time, and in movement. The task of a mise-en-scène is the spatial expression of the characters' inner and external behavior. Sergei Eisenstein called it "the director's gesture exploded in space." The search for the aesthetically generalized content of a mise-en-scène is, in fact, the director's effort to express individual psychology in space, time, and movement. Every separate fact must become an idea. The most complex ideas in the performance must be visualized through the actor's behavior in space. Actors who move on stage for such simple motivations as "I went to close the door" or "to greet someone" do not project true psychological reasoning. Space must be used for realization of the essence of the character.

Though we should not be tempted by what is merely

fashionable, unconventional means will not necessarily hurt the truthfulness of the action. Sometimes an unconventional approach may reveal an idea in a more expressive way. Our aim is to reflect man's destiny, his relationships with his environment, his conflicts, sufferings, and joys.

Make certain that you don't let anything on stage escape your attention. The composition of the performance is the director's basic task. He must be capable of defining the relationship between the parts and the whole.

The director must excite his actors with his ideas. Precision and verbal imagery will help you share your ideas with the actors. But to be able to verbalize in a picturesque way does not mean that you know how to realize your ideas. Even if you know what you want to build, it is no guarantee that you know how to build it. And yet the most important thing in the director's profession is to realize what lives within him and stirs him.

Vision and its realization are the essential qualities of a director's work. The director may have the intent but remain unable to realize it. And sometimes there is realization of a performance but no intent. This is not always the fault of the director. It may occur when the director is hindered by actors who are not ready to fulfill his vision. The director then loses time training actors in basic technique. The standard of the performance must, of course, suffer. The director becomes a teacher. Transforming a rehearsal into a class does not help the director or the performance.

Performance is the visual incarnation of the action in space and in time. The director must have a feeling for the plastic in space. The play becomes visual when the space "speaks" to the director and when actors are not indifferent to how they move in relation to their partners and to objects on stage. The form flows from the intent, and the director must "see" it before the set designer "sees" it. The director should excite the set designer with his ideas. Otherwise a conflict may arise which will destroy the integrity of the performance. Sets are an active force in the performance. Stanislavski said, "Designers are very sensitive people; we must tear out their ideas the way we pull out a bad tooth—not with a single pull, but by shaking it little by little, and then without their noticing, remove it."

Another important and active element in the performance is music. As in ancient times, music in twentieth-century theatre becomes a contributing part of the action. From merely being illustrative, music has become a means capable of condensing the drama and of bringing a level of generalization that is hardly possible through other means. One of the most important tasks of a director is the creation of an atmosphere on stage. Music creates a special theatre atmosphere. It is capable of influencing the course of an action; it can make the action continuous. If the director is capable of inner vision and sees his intent in images, he will be aware of the utility of his inner "hearing" of music. If he has a feeling for contemporary times, he will know what music can do for his production and how to incorporate its specific composition into the mise-en-scène.

Music has an exceptional ability to reflect the life of the human spirit and transmit it in a beautiful and artistic form. Music increases the emotional effect of the actor's performance on the audience without allowing itself to merge completely with the action on stage. Music may become the most important emotional factor in a production. Such use of music as an active participant in the movement of the action serves the superobjective.

■ ■ ■

Aristotle said that conflict is the basis and the soul of drama. Another philosopher, Hegel, said: "Dramatic action does not consist in simply walking toward your aim without encountering any obstacles on the way. On the contrary, it is rooted in obstacles, in the colliding passions of the characters."

Although Stanislavski did not formulate the rules for directing, his approach in practice is quite clear: "Make sure that the idea of the play is firmly on the ground. The idea of the play must struggle with the environment, with people of different disposition, with the events. Let them fight it. The idea will be born, it will triumph through the fierce struggle." Moreover, when an actor steps onto the stage, he has only one objective: to struggle.

When there is no conflict, there is no drama. The director's material is struggle. And his art will depend on his ability to unite everyone in that struggle.

Conflicts and contradictions are the motivating force and the kernel of the dramatic work. The director must be capable of revealing the knot of dramatic contradictions and the psychological states of the characters. He must find the inner logic of the contradictions and trace ways to overcome them. Every play presents a chain of changing human relationships, and the director must bring out the essence of these relationships in a theatrical image.

In every play there is a collision of the through line of actions with its opposite. The outcome of the struggle must be revealed through subordinate struggles, each for a concrete object. The most significant theme will be lost if it is not revealed in struggles for concrete objects. The object of a struggle is what takes place on stage in the given episode; it is the center of attention of all who take part in the struggle, although their strivings and motivations may differ.

The analysis of the play should first focus on ideas concerning the basic conflict, on the ways of incarnating it, and the determination of the subordinate conflicts. Analysis through events and actions, which you have been learning, is obligatory during rehearsals.

Expressiveness does not depend merely on the aims of the characters, but on the importance of these aims. Every objective must be completely fulfilled before one proceeds to the next one. Details must be thoroughly selected and expressed in a sculptural way. Such details will help the harmony of the whole, which is subordinated to a certain rhythm. Even a fully lifelike detail may carry meaningful weight and become a metaphor. Nothing accidental should occur on stage unless it is inspired.

The director must be capable of mercilessly eliminating anything that is superfluous, even if it is the most original idea he has ever had. The great Chaliapin said, "Emotions, intonations, and gestures must be expressed according to exact measurements corresponding to the given character and the given situation."

The mise-en-scène is the visual plastic expression of the states, conflicts, and interactions of the characters. It should not be invented; it is born when the struggle is vividly clear. The mise-en-scène arises as a concrete form of the solution for the given episode.

The director will have found the solution of the performance when he has understood what is most important in the whole play, in every scene and in every role. The director gives meaningful content to the contradiction as it evolves.

The director must make the theme concrete. The concretization of the theme is at the same time the motivation of its events. The clarity of the principal object of struggle depends on motivation. The struggle in process points to the main theme and its significance. While leading the struggle, the character moves to his objective. The obstacles that he encounters stall him, and this reveals his essence. P.M. Ershov, the eminent Russian scholar of theatre and Stanislavski, says, "The struggle is a spectacle of experiences. The most meaningful are the experiences that are visual." The struggle, he says, is "the polyphony of actions," and the director resembles the conductor who is also the composer of the libretto.

I wish to remind you of Stanislavski's words: "The inner technique which is essential for the correct creative state is based on the person's willpower. This is why so many actors are deaf to my appeals. I had hundreds of students but only a few could be called my followers, and only a few understand the goal to which I dedicated my life." I hope that you understand Stanislavski's goal—at least some of you.

If you are an innovator, you may be isolated, since

recognition may come only in the future.

Though the director has no right to have "moods," you do not have to be afraid of your actors. One young Russian director confessed that his first rehearsal frightened him more than the war. Nemirovich-Danchenko, the great director, said, "Though the director at times may be the actor's servant, may have to adjust to the personality of the set designer and take into account the demands from the management, in the end the director is the master of the performance."

■ Class Twelve
The Playwright

Pat: I knew when I started your course that my work as an actress was going to improve, but now I'm experiencing a fringe benefit that I hadn't expected. The play I've been writing has started to flow and make sense in a whole new way. I'm sure it's because the entire idea of a play has changed for me in your classes.

S.M.: I have purposely delayed telling you how Stanislavski helps the playwright. I wanted you to first assimilate enough of the technique. Until now, our discussion would have been only theoretical. Now that you understand the System organically, you'll know why Stanislavski thought that playwrights do not give the actor enough nourishment. He said, "Authors often fail to find the deep inner action which crosses the character's psychology, and so they substitute an external schematic line. I often do not feel that there is a vast world behind the stage, and that what happens on stage is only a part of it. The characters often do not have their biographies, and that is very important for an actor."

Great achievement is rare in any art; only rarely is there a playwright who is able to give us a full idea of the biography of his characters. The playwright is responsible for their destinies. Otherwise even good actors may have difficulty in building major characters. A bad play hurts the actor's and director's art, pushing them into clichés.

A good play must have an important idea, sharp conflicts, and concrete, clearly delineated characters. A play will never be valid without these elements, which must be disclosed through events as well as the behavior of the characters.

Writers, Stanislavski said, must know the organic laws of nature and the way they are used on stage. Stanislavski believed in Pushkin's demand for both dramatists and actors: "Truth of passions, truth of experience in given circumstances." They must also know that events are the stimuli for actions. Therefore a good playwright builds events and establishes their influence on his characters and their actions.

Stanislavski advises the playwright to build his play through significant intense events because the actions of the characters depend on them. A good playwright goes through all the thinking of his characters to establish each one's individuality. Maxim Gorki said, "If you have the characters, you have the material for unavoidable drama. Put these characters in front of each other, and they will act at once." If a playwright has an important idea, his theme will create a natural interweaving of events and the conflicts that result from it. Conflicts are built from the struggle of ideas, and should be expressed through the characters' actions. The more significance a dramatist gives the events and the actions of the characters, the sharper the play becomes.

The dramatist should take his characters from real

life. The spectators want to see people like themselves, with ambitions, thoughts, passions—all the behavior of real life in the process of either growth or retrogression.

The playwright should foresee psychological pauses. You know a great deal now about the inner monologue. A talented dramatist can imply intense inner monologue. A well-filled pause will disclose the subtext. Then, as in Chekhov's plays, the characters will answer each other's thoughts. A good playwright does not have one superfluous word. This is why I stressed the importance to you, the actors, of projecting everything you say.

The superobjective and the through line of actions are most important for a playwright. The through line of actions, the undercurrent of the life of the play, moves the inner world of the characters. A playwright should avoid any detail that does not help the through line of actions to disclose the superobjective. If a playwright knows the Stanislavski System as you do, he will know that the through line of actions can continue its movement in the thoughts of the character's mind.

Every action must have a counteraction that will strengthen and sharpen it. There should be clashes between contradictory forces. The deep emotional response of the spectators depends on the depth of the conflict.

Now, Pat, in addition to what I have said, your language in the play must be poetic and also reflect your own individuality. It will be active and poetic if you, the dramatist, are able to move the through line of actions as the undercurrent of your play in such a way that it will stir the images of the actor and of the spectator. You must write in strong and picturesque language. If you want the speech in your play to be musical, the tempo-rhythm must be taken into consideration.

All events on stage must be important, but you must give special emphasis to:

1. the first event, which begins the through line of actions and explains the beginning relationships in a play;

2. the central event, which is the stimulus for the through line of actions;

3. the final event, which either brings about the solution of the conflict or shows the impossibility of a solution.

A dramatist or director should not be afraid of a strong and dramatic finale.

Stanislavski's suggestions for playwrights will be useful to you when you write a play, but when it is staged—though you as the author will be most important—give the director independence in his field. Sometimes the director and the actors bring out depths that the author himself has not suspected.

You have learned how much the Stanislavski technique depends on a friendly and harmonious atmosphere in the group. His system is inseparable from his ethical principles. You must remember that the theatre's aim is not merely simplicity but the creation of profoundly *alive* characters who help to make the idea of the play clear. The goal of the Stanislavski System is to involve the actor's organic nature in the building of a character. The Stanislavski System will bring the actor to that intangible state in which he creates subconsciously. His attitude toward the world around him changes. His rhythm becomes that of a new man.

■ Suggested Exercises

The following are some of the exercises that we use at the beginning of each class at the Sonia Moore Studio.

■ RELAXATION OF MUSCLES EXERCISES

• Rise. Make fists. Stand on your toes. Tense your whole body as if you are holding a heavy burden. Throw your load on a high shelf or hang it on a hook.

Exhale, sit, and relax your muscles completely. Lean back in the chair.

Inhale again. Tense only the necessary muscles. Sit in a free but disciplined pose, withyour head up and your back straight, without leaning on your chair.

Sit in a pose that will permit you to jump up at the teacher's signal. Repeat the whole cycle of the above exercise.

The rhythm of the exercise must be strictly in accord with the rhythm of your breathing; this is especially important for achieving the correct result.

• To check normal tension: Sit or stand and check from your head to your toes that the tension of your body is in its natural state.

First check the muscles of your face. Some actors

involuntarily raise their eyebrows or bring them together, narrow their eyes, widen their lips, or smile artificially. This should be eliminated, if necessary, with the help of a mirror.

Often the shoulders are raised from nervousness. You must learn to relax. Let your arms hang loosely and flex your wrists. Be aware of your spine and free it from unnecessary firmness and limpness.

Relax your knees, legs, feet.

- To achieve a plastic walk: Walk on your toes.

- Lie on the floor and relax your muscles. Raise one leg and hug it at the knee. If the muscles are relaxed, the leg will bend easily and the foot will slide along the floor before being lifted. If the foot remains at a stiff angle, make circles in the air and wiggle your toes. Repeat with other foot.

- To free involuntary tension in the arms: Let your arm hang freely and loosely. Tense and relax the muscles of the arm. Repeat with other arm.

  To check relaxation: The teacher or another student grasps a finger and raises the arm slowly, then lets it down slowly. The hand should be completely relaxed and subordinate to the movements, without helping or hindering. Again the arm is raised and quickly let go. The arm should fall, with a slight bend at the elbow.

- Tense your right arm and left leg and then relax them. Tense your left arm and right leg and relax them.

- Increase or expand movement of the arms by imagining that muscular energy is flowing through the arm from the shoulder to the fingertips. Shrink a movement by imagining that the flow is reversed. Practice with such gestures as necessary for saying "Look here!" and "Come here!" at first slowly and then more quickly.

The above exercises each should be justified by objectives and circumstances.

Muscular control, when it becomes second nature, will be a great help during the creative process.

Stanislavski demanded precise sequences and graduality in moving from one position to another. Dissect any movement into its intermediary links and become aware of how the muscular energy progresses. Fulfill the whole movement slowly while consciously controlling the muscles. Then direct full attention to the action. Know your objective and build the circumstances. Strive for a psychophysical state in each situation.

- Reach for an object.

- Pick a fruit from a tree.

- Rise from a prone position.

- Lie down to rest.

- Bend to see something on the ground and straighten to see something over your head.

- Sit, rise, walk.

- Throw out each finger in turn, then all the fingers together. Gradually bend every joint. Relax the whole hand and let it fall loosely, shaking it as if there were dough on it that you wanted to be rid of. Turn the hand, making circles in the air to one side, then the other. Sweep the hand up and touch imaginary silk or velvet. Repeat with the other hand.

• Repeat the above exercise using approximately the same movements for the feet. Throw one leg over another and exercise each foot separately.

• Relax the muscles of your face and body. Lie down. You are relaxed and fall asleep. Waking up, you realize that you are sinking into mud, which is like glue. Wonder, evaluate. Make a decision and a meaningful gesture. Then try to pull out of the mud. The movement of pulling out preceded by the steps (wondering, evaluating, deciding—with an expressive gesture before you move and another when you stop moving) becomes transformed into physical action. The gesture when you stop moving may be a reflex of the gesture you made before starting your movement out of the mud. While you are immobile your objective may change (you may think of a better way to save yourself). A new action begins and you again wonder, etc.

In the following group exercises the teacher or group leader should suggest objectives and circumstances.

- Change seats noiselessly.

- Make a circle and sit without noise.

- Make two rows and sit noiselessly.

- Repeat the above exercises with your eyes closed.

- Repeat the above exercises in different tempo-rhythms, possibly with music which suggests, in addition to tempo, the character of the movements.

Any change in the sets on stage, the position of the furniture, etc. should be considered as exercises in precision, organization, lightness, noiselessness, and quickness of action. To learn to make changes on stage before an audience, repeat the above in the dark.

- Sing a song in your mind. At the teacher's signal, sing it aloud. At another signal, sing it again in your mind. Concentrate on your own song while others are singing.

- All sing the same song together. At the teacher's signal, all continue it in their minds. At another signal, one or two sing it aloud.

- While others are singing:
    multiply
    say a few lines of a poem
    read an article in a paper and be able to tell about it.

- Compete for quickness in:
    touching as many objects as you can

> naming as many cities as you can
> naming as many famous persons as you can.

- Note what is new about a student today.

- Tell with great detail an episode in your life.

- Name all the objects of the same color in a room.

- Name objects beginning with a particular letter of the alphabet.

- Recreate precisely the pose and movement of a colleague.

- Leave the room while changes are made in the room. Return and describe the changes with thorough and specific details.

- Look into the eyes of a colleague. Turn away and describe their color, expression, form. Check whether you were right.

- Listen to the noises outside. Tell what kind of car passed in the street.

- Listen to sounds in the building.

- Listen to another student's speech. Reproduce his intonations, his pronunciation, and include any defects in his diction.

- Listen to music. Tell about the images and feelings it stirs. Explain how the composer achieves this using melody, rhythm, dynamics and tone.

- Touch a fabric with your eyes closed and identify it.

- Touch an object with your eyes closed and describe its form. Identify it.

- Touch a person's clothes or hands with your eyes closed and identify him.

- Say a word. A second person repeats it and adds another. A third repeats the first two and adds a third, etc.

An actor must, above all, develop the ability to see in detail the peculiarities of human behavior in different circumstances. He must perceive the inner logic and dynamics of the events that take place.

- Outside of class, observe people, guessing their profession and disposition.

- Outside of class, observe the relationships between people and be able to explain them in class.

- Attract the attention of a particular person in the room.

- Stand up, turn to your chair, bend, pick up the chair, raise it, put it down, turn and sit. All movements must be light, quiet, precise.

More Advanced Group Exercises

- Stand in line for a newspaper and discover that all the papers have been sold.

- Several persons at a time walk or run through the stage. They stop and see something on their left or right. Those who watch decide which group was more expressive and better understood. They will be better understood if the lights are turned off and the spectators are allowed to see each group for only a few seconds.

- All except two persons (one male, one female) leave the

room. These two create a living picture. Those who have left enter by twos and observe the tableau for five seconds. They recreate the pose of their colleagues and compete for the most accurate depiction. Decide which couple was able to recreate the scene most accurately.

In the following exercises, the central action is the same for all, but each actor has a different task and thus a different logic of behavior.

- Imagine you are in a bus. Observe one another without being noticed. Turn your backs and describe one another's appearance.

- Imagine you are arriving at a reception. Everyone comes on stage, orients himself, sees the hosts, greets them and meets other guests. Find the most justified and convenient position on stage. If someone blocks you, find a way out. Try to arrange yourselves as if on a chessboard.

- Imagine that you are:
    on a picnic in a field
    resting on a beach
    at work in the fields
    at a table deciding on the composition of a paper.

- Go to a window to see a catastrophe in the street. Some strive to see it while others avoid seeing it. One is explaining what has happened.

- Imagine that you are in a fishermen's village, waiting for relatives to return after a storm.
    Repeat with music.

- Recreate a scene in a painting or sculpture. Include the moment which preceded it and one which could follow it.

- Recreate Leonardo da Vinci's "The Last Supper."

- Imagine that you are in a doll store.

- Imagine that you are in a farmyard.

- Imagine that you are at a party in another era. Concentrate on etiquette, handling a fan or cane, etc.

- Each person takes his chair and brings it to the center of the room. All form a circle facing outward.

  Change this circle at the teacher's command into two parallel rows, still facing outward.

  At the command of the teacher, the two rows exchange places, all moving simultaneously without losing the precise pattern of the movement. Repeat with music.

- Repeat the above exercise while the teacher makes a sound (raps on the table, etc.) and keep track of the number of sounds made.

- A first person names an adjective, a second person a noun, a third person a verb—in that order. This is repeated, and a logical story must be made up from the sentences.

- The "typewriter." Each person is assigned a letter of the alphabet. The teacher dictates a sentence and it is "typed" as each person claps when his letter comes up. All clap together at the end of every word.

- Repeat the above exercise, dividing the class into two

groups and typing in a synchronized tempo.

• Repeat the above exercise, dividing the class into two groups. Each group "types" the text independently, competing for speed and precision.

• Each person takes his chair and runs around the room in a circle. At the teacher's command, the direction is reversed without collisions or noise.

At another signal, the chairs are placed in the center of the room, forming a pyramid, while running in a circle is continued.

At a third signal, each person pulls his chair from the pyramid. If it is covered with other chairs, make another run around the circle.

Finally, all put their chairs in place, sit, and freeze.

■ SILENT EXERCISES AND IMPROVISATIONS

When doing the following exercises, know your objective, build the circumstances, and make sure that both are clear to the audience. Since these exercises are silent, the actor must have a continuous inner monologue, that consists of wondering, evaluating, and making decisions. Use the muscles in your torso to stir an inner monologue. Make a gesture expressing your state of mind before and after each physical action. Never stop striving for psycho-physical unity.

- Thoroughly examine an object.

- Listen to a sound.

- Search for something.

- Read.

- Memorize a few lines.

- Repeat the above exercises while moving through a room for a specific purpose: to pick up something, to ask a question, etc.

- Pour a glass of water and give it to someone.

- Say good-bye to a place.

- Change the position of the furniture, following the teacher's instructions.

- Open a window.

- Close a window.

- Silently count the number of bulbs in the ceiling.

- Watch the shore coming closer from the deck of a ship.

- Go on stage through the auditorium. Justify and add circumstances: rain, a vicious dog, etc.

Active action always presupposes the overcoming of an obstacle. There is no scenic creativity without contradictions, conflicts, or struggle.

- Open a door.

- Close a door.

- Sit
    in court
    in order to be photographed.

- Justify and connect three movements.

- Approach a friend to:
    tell him bad news
    borrow money
    steal from him
    surprise him.

- Read
    at home
    in your own room
    in a waiting room
    in a library.

- Pack.

- Search your roommate's bureau.

- Come to tell a friend important news. He is not at home.

- As you are leaving for a party
    - discover the loss of a piece of jewelry or your wallet
    - receive a note with bad news.

- Come home
    - to work
    - to rest
    - from working in a mine.

- Burn
    - a letter
    - secret material.

- Rent an apartment.

- Take the wrong train.

- Awake and find your room empty.

- Watch over a sick person. Influence others to be quiet so as not to disturb him.

- Wait for an ambulance.

- Examine a watch stolen from you.

- Tell without words of something you saw in the street.

- Get ready for work:
    - You cannot find a book you need.
    - Your shoe heel breaks.
    - Your watch stops.

- Open a door because you heard hard knocking. There is no one there.

- Enter a room
  - to hide
  - to meet an unknown person
  - in the dark to steal something.

- Try to make an important phone call. The phones are out of order.

- Try to understand a telegraph message.

- Try on a new jacket
  - as a theatrical costume
  - which is too big.

- Shake hands with different persons.

- Enter, stand on a chair, go to your knees on the floor, run out.

- Search for an object that the teacher has hidden. Repeat the search, knowing where the object is hidden.

- Clean a room
  - for yourself
  - for your employers.

- Eavesdrop.

- Wait for a diagnosis.

- Treat
  - a shawl as a cat
  - a chair as a vicious dog
  - a chair as a throne
  - a chair as an electric chair
  - a bottle as an antique
  - a bottle as a milk bottle

a liquid as poison
a liquid as hot tea
a liquid as cold water.

Silent Exercises with Two or More People.

- At the bed of a patient, talk to others with gestures.

- Two people are in a room together
  after a quarrel
  who are not on speaking terms.

- Two are at the opera. A third disturbs them because one of their faces is familiar.

- Two are spies, a third is a detective.

- Play the first moment in various unexpected meetings. Have contact with your partner, have a definite relationship, analyze the logic of behavior.

■ SENSE MEMORY EXERCISES

An actor, in addition to observing life and its phenomena, must preserve in his memory different sensations and observations. Sense memory is the ability to recreate in your mind images of real life. Sense memory influences emotional memory. Memory of previous sensations must be developed. This is closely connected with thinking on stage and seeing images.

There must be precision and concreteness in the memories of previously experienced sensations. To verify this, you make sketch an image, express a sculpture with your body or block out a painting with others' bodies.

- Describe:
    the interior of an apartment you know
    a painting by an important painter
    a well-known building
    the looks of a colleague.

- Remember your first impression of seeing the sea: waves rolling, the taste of salt water, etc.

- Remember the sound of:
    the wind
    rain
    thunder
    a bird singing.

- Remember the timbre
    of a voice you know
    of a popular melody.

- Remember the taste of
    mustard
    lemon
    wine.

- Remember the sensation of:
    cold water
    hot water
    a toothache
    bitterly cold weather
    a hot day.

- Imagine that the class is taking place in the garden: it is beginning to rain, there are mosquitos, etc.

- Answer a question while you have a toothache which you are hiding.

- Remember the sensation of having something in your eye.

- Talk while thinking of sentimental music.

- Cross a room in a museum.

- Pick mushrooms.

- Enter a room to which you have been summoned to give an explanation: it is night, during a bombardment, etc.

- Describe your most pleasant experience.

- Describe a person you met in the street.

■ EXERCISES WITH IMAGINARY OBJECTS

These exercises must be done to perfection. They may be divided into two groups:

Group I—Those requiring the effort of the whole body or large groups of muscles, large movements of the arms and legs, or bending and unbending the whole body:

- Make a bed.

- Clean a room.

- Wash the floor.

- Do the laundry.

- Move imaginary objects of different weights and forms.

- Dig in the ground.
- Plant a tree.
- Open a theatrical curtain.
- Bowl.
- Hang a picture.
- Pack a suitcase.

Group II—Those in which the fingers and hands are primarily active:

- Thread a needle.
- Make a salad.
- Scramble eggs.
- Decorate a Christmas tree.
- Wash yourself.
- Dress.
- Sew.
- Handle a lock, keys, money.
- Prepare clay and make a figure.
- Peel a hot potato.
- Peel a hot egg.
- Thread beads.

Exercises with imaginary objects may be performed by several persons at the same time. Everyone should fulfill his own task, while all have the same action:

- Meet at a dinner table.

- Work in a factory.

- Work in a store with customers.

- Make a portrait of a student with imaginary paints or charcoal using real paper.

■ EXERCISES FOR IMAGES

Make sure you achieve psychophysical unity before you speak. Compete for the involvement of those who listen. Ask your listeners what they have in their minds as they hear what is being told.

- Tell what you did this morning.

- Tell your most interesting experience yesterday with minute details.

- Look at a picture, describe it, justify what is happening in it.

- Tell about a show, a film, a trip in some special given circumstances: for example, tell about an event in your life in order to warn a friend, tell about a play to defend it against criticism.

- Describe a street through which you often walk. Compare it with other streets—this will bring out what is unique about it.

- Describe
    a cloud
    a star
    a room.

- Explain a phrase, a story.

■ TEMPO-RHYTHM EXERCISES

• Sit, stand in different rhythms.

• Search for an object in different tempos.

• Listen, look over some objects, think, try to remember.

Tempo-Rhythm Exercises with Imaginary Objects

• Write a letter.

• Dress.

• Set the table.

• While dressing, notice that your watch has stopped. Change the tempo-rhythm but slow down again when you realize that you are already late.

Two Different Tempo-Rhythms Simultaneously

• You are depressed by tragic news but are trying to hide it and be gay.

• You are ready to dance from happiness, but must keep yourself calm for some reason.

• Group scenes using a metronome—the central action is the same for all, but each has a different task:
    a dance
    a party
    a store
    a railway station.

• Listen to music. Determine the images, associations, circumstances that arise within the melody.

In performing the preceding exercise, do not be passive; fulfill the actions in circumstances. The music must be translated into the language of actions. If the imagination does not respond at first, fulfill the simplest action: approach a table, sit, stand, leave a book, etc., while strictly observing the tempo.

■ ORAL EXERCISES AND IMPROVISATIONS

Psychophysical unity must be achieved in order to fulfill a verbal action. When doing these exercises, the actor must go through each of the steps of an action (wondering, evaluating, etc.) before he speaks followed by a gesture after he speaks.

• Give signals as a commander: "Get up," "Forward," etc.

• Invite a girl to dance. Be aware of your body.

• Go through a crowd to a seat in a bus. You may have to say: "I beg your pardon."

• As a policeman, stop a man who violated traffic regulations.

• Cross a street against the light. A policeman stops you but you have a serious reason to hurry. He insists that you pay a fine.

• Improvise, based on the following actions:

ask forgiveness	make fun of
blackmail	persuade
call	push

compare	question
compete	reproach
embarrass	ridicule
encourage	show off
find out	stop
flirt	surprise
frighten	surrender
humiliate	threaten
lie	warn

- Borrow money from someone in a crowd because you suddenly realize that you haven't enough money to get home.

- Approach a person to
  become acquainted
  ask for an autograph.

- Greet a person
  who hurt you
  whom you respect
  whom you think you are superior to
  to amuse him.

- Become acquainted with someone
  while hiding a headache
  while hiding a tragedy.

- Read a letter
  as a professor
  as an illiterate person.

- You are caring for a sick person in another room. Your brother enters and loudly asks questions. Command him to be quiet and tell him what has happened when he insists on going into the sickroom; you try to keep him out.

• You are approached by a gangster on the street. You try to escape into a building, but the doorman will not let you in.

• Return money you have borrowed from a friend. He does not want to accept it because he knows you are in a difficult situation. Leave the money where he does not see it and leave the room.

• Arrive in New York for the first time. You expect someone to meet you, but no one is there.

• Attempt to make peace with a girl you have offended silently, as if there are other people in the room.

• Talk about the weather
   as two people who have just met
   as two persons in love
   at the beginning of a long separation
   at a truce after a quarrel
   during a first walk after a long illness
   in an unexpected encounter on the street
   during a meeting of two conspirators.

• Your telephone rings. In answering it you can say only "Oh", "Well," "Yes," "No," "Hmm." Those who watch you must understand through your physical behavior your attitude to what you hear and how you feel about the person with whom you speak.

• Two persons who love each other must separate for an important reason. One is packing, the other is setting the table. Each can say only three sentences, and they are about the weather.

- A prisoner is convicted of murder. His mother comes to see him. He waits for her to tell him the result of his appeal. She knows that he was rejected but is unable to tell him. Each can only say three sentences—but not about what is on their minds.

- The teacher writes on pieces of paper such sentences as:

  "The weather is wonderful."
  "Yes, it has been a long time since we had such a nice day."
  "August was bad, but September has been good."

Each student draws one sentence and must use it in an improvisation. Exchange sentences and repeat.

Group Oral Exercises and Improvisations

- All imagine they are waiting for a train to depart. Each one has a different task: engineer, passengers, porters, ice cream sellers, etc.

- Two or three play cards. One of the players is interested in a conversation between two others on a couch.

- Act out themes from fairy tales.

- All imagine they are in a bus depot. A bus arrives at the depot, and one passenger awakes and realizes that he has overslept his station. He attempts to convince the driver to drive him where he must go. The driver resists because that would be against the law, but finally gives in.

Bibliography

"About Vera Maretzkaya." *VTO* (Moscow), 1985.

Batalov, A. "Destiny and Trade." *Art* (Moscow), 1984.

Bondarchuk, Sergei. "Desire for a Miracle." *The Young Guard* (Moscow), 1984.

Bordonov, G. "Molière." *Art* (Moscow), 1983.

"Culture of Speech on Stage and Films." *Science* (Moscow), 1986.

Efros, Anatoly. "Continuation of Theatre Story." *Art* (Moscow), 1985.

"Forms of Art in the Socialist Artistic Culture." *Art* (Moscow), 1984. [Collective monography]

Gorovich, B. "Opera Theatre." *Musika* (Leningrad), 1984.

Morov, A.G. "Three Centuries of Russian Stage." *Prosvenchenie* (Moscow), 1984.

"Myths and Reality." *Art* (Moscow), 1984.

"N.P. Okhlopkov." *VTO* (Moscow), 1986. [Articles and reminiscences]

Pimenov, V. "Time of Problems and Worries." *Soviet Writer* (Moscow), 1983.

Serebriakoff, Nikita N. "World Significance of Stanislavski." *Art* (Moscow), 1988.

Sharov, E.G. "Directing Cabaret and Mass Performances." *Prosveschenie* (Moscow), 1986.

Simonov, P.V. and P.M. Ershov. "Temperament. Character. Personality." *Nauka* (Moscow), 1984.

Streller, Georgio. "Theatre for People." *Raduga* (Moscow), 1984.

"Theatre Problems." *VTO* (Moscow), 1986. [Articles]

Theatre Magazine, monthly through 1990.

Turovskaya, M. "Babanova, Legend and Biography." *Art* (Moscow), 1981.

"Vladimir Iv. Nemirovich-Danchenko: About the Creativity of an Actor." *Art* (Moscow), 1984.

Zorkaya, N. "Alexei Popov." *Art* (Moscow), 1983, 1986.

A Brief Chronology of Stanislavski

1863   Born Konstantin Sergeevich Alexeev, in Moscow, January 5.

1877   Made his debut on his family's stage in an amateur show, September 5.

1885   Adopted the pseudonym Stanislavski.

1888   With director A.F. Fedotov, singer and teacher F.P. Kommisarjevski, and painter F.L. Sologub, Stanislavski founded the Society of Art and Literature and created a drama company of amateur actors associated with it.

1891   His first important independent directing work: Leo Tolstoi's *The Fruits of Enlightenment*.

1897   He had his famous encounter with Vladimir Nemirovich-Danchenko, during which they decided to found a theatre company of the most talented members of the Society of Art and Literature and Nemirovich-Danchenko's students in the Drama School of the Moscow Philharmonic Society. The company was to become the Moscow Art Theatre.

1898   The Moscow Art Theatre opened with a historical tragedy, Alexei Tolstoi's *Czar Feodor Ivanovich*, on October 4.
        The Moscow Art Theatre gave a production of Chekhov's *The Seagull*, directed by Stanislavski and Nemirovich-Danchenko, on December 5. The play, a triumphant success, heralded the true birth of the theatre and of a great playwright.

1900s   Stanislavski began to formulate his teachings on an actor's creativity known as the Stanislavski System.

1918   Became head of the Bolshoi Theatre's Opera Studio,

which later developed into the independent Opera Theatre of K.S. Stanislavski.

1928   During his performance as Vershinin in *The Three Sisters* on October 29, Stanislavski suffered a heart attack. After this he abandoned acting and concentrated on directing and on educating young actors and directors while continuing his search for the best acting techniques.

1930s   Stanislavski made new discoveries in the method of creating a performance and a role; it later became known as the method of physical actions.

1935   Founded the Opera-Drama Studio.

1938   Died in Moscow on August 7.

MONOLOGUE WORKSHOP

From Search to Discovery
in Audition and Performance
by Jack Poggi

To those for whom the monologue has always been synonymous with terror, *The Monologue Workshop* will prove an indispensable ally. Jack Poggi's new book answers the long-felt need among actors for top-notch guidance in finding, rehearsing, and performing monologues. For those who find themselves groping for a speech just hours before their "big break," this book is their guide to salvation.

The Monologue Workshop supplies the tools to discover new pieces before they become over-familiar, excavate older material that has been neglected, and adapt material from non-dramatic sources (novels, short stories, letters, diaries, autobiographies, even newspaper columns). There are also chapters on writing original monologues and creating solo performances in the style of Lily Tomlin and Eric Bogosian.

Besides the wealth of practical advice he offers, Poggi transforms the monologue experience from a terrifying ordeal into an exhilarating opportunity. Jack Poggi, as many working actors will attest, is the actor's partner in a process they had always thought was without one.

paper • ISBN: 1-55783-031-2

SHAKESCENES
SHAKESPEARE FOR TWO
Edited with an Introduction
by John Russell Brown

Shakespeare's plays are not the preserve of "Shakespearean Actors" who specialize in a remote species of dramatic life. John Russell Brown offers guidance for those who have little or no experience with the formidable Bard in both the Introduction and Advice to Actors, and in the notes to each of the thirty-five scenes.

The scenes are presented in newly-edited texts, with notes which clarify meanings, topical references, puns, ambiguities, etc. Each scene has been chosen for its independent life requiring only the simplest of stage properties and the barest of spaces. A brief description of characters and situation prefaces each scene, and is followed by a commentary which discusses its major acting challenges and opportunities.

Shakescenes are for small classes and large workshops, and for individual study whenever two actors have the opportunity to work together.

From the Introduction:

"Of course, a way of speaking a character's lines meaningfully and clearly must be found, but that alone will not bring any play to life. Shakespeare did not write for talking heads ... Actors need to be acutely present all the time; ... they are like boxers in a ring, who dare not lose concentration or the ability to perform at full power for fear of losing consciousness altogether."

paper • ISBN: 1-55783-049-5